When you give someone a book,
you don't give him just paper, ink, and glue.
You give him the possibility of a whole new life.
–Christopher Morley, novelist, journalist, and poet

Praise for
It's All Part of the Dance
Finding Happiness in an Upside Down World
by Alan Gettis, Ph.D.

"Full of insight and passion, *It's All Part of the Dance* is a great gift to each of us. It is a remarkable guide to living a happier and more fulfilling life. I loved it. Dr. Gettis has an engaging writing style that is both entertaining and enlightening. You'll be grateful that you treated yourself to this book. Buy two copies and give one to a friend. You'll be happy you did."

> –Harvey McKinnon, bestselling author of *The Power of Giving: How Giving Back Enriches Us All*

"Fasten your seatbelt as Dr. Alan Gettis fearlessly takes the reader into his own intimate and personal world of chaos, pathos, awe, and awakening. Weaving the myriad threads of a lifetime of self-exploration, *It's All Part of the Dance* offers a simple, elegant, thoroughly enjoyable tour-de-force for finding true and lasting joy, purpose and meaning. Regardless of your life circumstance, you quickly begin to recognize that you and me and Dr. Gettis — we're all part of a dance ... the very same dance! Read this book — I guarantee you'll finally begin to hear life's music."

> –Joseph J. Luciani, Ph.D., bestselling author of *Reconnecting: A Self-Coaching Solution to Revive Your Love Life*

"I only have three words to describe Alan Gettis's book and they are WOW, WOW, WOW!!! I could not put the book down. On a scale of 1 to 5, I would give this book a 20. It is a must read for anyone who wants to find true happiness."

> –Michael Monji, author of *Does It Pay to Die?*

"I challenge you to find a more comprehensive, well-organized volume of parables and inspiring stories on the art of living well than this one. In *It's All Part of the Dance*, Alan Gettis shows us how to find happiness in an upside down world. He really gets it. Not only does he get it, he eloquently illustrates how you can too. This book works on many levels. There is nothing esoteric or pedantic about it. Reading like a novel, it is easy to become engrossed in the stories — yet each page reveals part of the secret of true happiness. Sometimes it is obvious, at other times more subtle. Do yourself a favor; read it once as quickly as you wish, then go back and spend time going through it slowly, savoring it and allowing your mind to absorb the essence of each story. Chock-full of concepts and ideas that you can use in your life today, *It's All Part of the Dance: Finding Happiness in an Upside Down World* gets my highest recommendation. Get the book and you too can 'get it' in this upside down world!"

–David Ambrose, author of *Your Life Manual: Practical Steps to Genuine Happiness*

"*It's All Part of the Dance* focuses on changing our individual perspective of all that surrounds us in our personal world and how we respond to it in order to become happier in life. Dr. Gettis guides readers through a wonderful journey of self-discovery by using personal stories, humor, quotes, and powerful insights. It's impossible to come away from this book without changing at least one negative perspective in your life. This is a must-read for everyone in today's ever changing world."

–Jennifer Chase, criminologist and author of *Compulsion*

"Whether you are beginning on the path to enlightenment or closing in on your goal, this book will be important to you. Have you ever had a dream about being able to fly? Remember the exhilaration you felt? *It's All Part of the Dance* aims to show you how to live in that constant state throughout your life. Highly recommended!"

–Donald A. Wilhelm, author of *This Time's a Charm:*
Lessons of a Four-Time Cancer Survivor

"In *It's All Part of the Dance*, Alan Gettis shows you that genuine happiness is only a stone's throw away. He teaches you how to get out of your own way and harness the unlimited potential of your mind and of the human spirit. Paradoxically, the book is both simple and profound as it weaves anecdotes, research, storytelling, science, and spirituality. The bottom line for me is that this book will make a real difference in how you feel and how you live your life. Highly recommended."

–Dr. Sam Menahem, author of *When Therapy Isn't Enough:*
The Healing Powers of Prayer and Psychotherapy

"While putting the responsibility for being happy squarely upon your shoulders, Dr. Gettis asks, 'Would you really want it any other way?' When the light bulb comes on and you really get it — that you are the problem and that you are the solution — it is empowering and liberating. *It's All Part of the Dance* is packed with rich insights and accessible wisdom that provide a road map to living the fulfilled life. Very highly recommended!"

–Dr. Aymee Coget, Sustainable Happiness Expert and
CEO of the American Happiness Association

"In *It's All Part of the Dance*, Alan Gettis shares a delicious collection of intimate, heartfelt reflections on life, love, and the pursuit of happiness. His stories and insights are charming, folksy, and intelligent—offered more in the spirit of a wise elder brother than a detached mental health professional. It's easy to read, entertaining, and profound. I felt like we were just sitting around the living room having a lovely, meaningful, enlightening conversation. I highly recommend this very precious, helpful book!"

–John E. Welshons, author of *One Soul, One Love,*
One Heart and *Awakening From Grief*

"This inspiring book provides a compassionate and sensitive blueprint for building resiliency, psychological integrity, and inner peace, which are important keys to happiness. Dr. Gettis suggests that instead of waiting for the storm to pass, we should learn to dance in the midst of it. *It's All Part of the Dance* is less about survival and playing it safe and more about 'showing up for your life' and embracing it passionately. If you value happiness, this is an invaluable book."

–Hueina Su, The Nurturer's Coach and bestselling author of
Intensive Care for the Nurturer's Soul: 7 Keys to Nurture
Yourself While Caring for Others

"If life's throwing you some unfair curves, read *It's All Part of the Dance*. Dr. Alan Gettis will teach you how to be more resilient to whatever is coming next on the road of life. This is an empowering book, filled with interesting research, Zen wisdom, and great tips to help you feel happier and more fulfilled."

–Beth Greer, author of *Super Natural Home*, holistic health
advocate, and radio show host

"Wow ... what a great book, especially for these times. I'm happy I read it."

   –Allan Hunkin, speaker, writer, broadcaster, and author of
   Finding the Elegant Solution In Any Situation

The Eric Hoffer Awards include the Montaigne Medal to honor books that "illuminate, progress, or redirect thought." *It's All Part of the Dance* was selected as one of the best books on the prestigious "short list" for the 2010 Montaigne Medal.

It's All Part of the Dance was honored as an award-winning finalist at the National Best Books Awards sponsored by USA Book News.

IT'S ALL PART
OF THE DANCE
Finding Happiness in an Upside Down World

Alan Gettis, Ph.D.

GOODMAN BECK PUBLISHING

GOODMAN BECK PUBLISHING

PO Box 253
Norwood, NJ 07648
www.goodmanbeck.com

ISBN 978-0-9798755-3-3

Library of Congress Control Number 2009933447

Printed in the United States of America

10 9 8 7 6 5 4 3 2 1

OTHER BOOKS BY ALAN GETTIS

The Happiness Solution:
Finding Joy and Meaning in an Upside Down World

Seven Times Down, Eight Times Up:
Landing on Your Feet in an Upside Down World—
Second Edition, Updated and Expanded

Sun Faced Haiku, Moon Faced Haiku

In the Beak of a Duck

Dedicated with love to
my favorite sister, Harriet,
and my big brother, Rip,
both of whom have made my life
more interesting and more meaningful.

CONTENTS

Acknowledgments   *xix*
Preface   *xxi*
Introduction   *1*
How Happy Are You?   *5*

I.   **ATTITUDE**   *11*
My First Ticonderoga   *13*
Life Is Bizarre   *15*
20,000 Moments   *17*
Max's Sandwich Shop   *20*
Putting It in Perspective   *23*
Never Say Never   *25*
How Do I Love Thee?   *28*
My Brother-In-Law   *31*
A Different Ball Game   *33*
The Humble Dog   *36*

II.   **CHOICES** *39*
        On Living in Potemkin Village *41*
        Let It Go *44*
        A History Lesson *46*
        The Stock Exchange *50*
        Say What *52*
        Two Cents *55*
        Me Me Me *57*
        Managing Your Life *59*
        Just a Dream *62*
        How Many Therapists Does It Take
          to Change a Lightbulb? *64*

III.   **THINKING & ATTENTION** *67*
        The Comparison Trap *69*
        Accentuate the Positive *72*
        Would You Like That Supersized? *75*
        Pull the Plug *77*
        Occam's Razor *79*
        AAA *82*
        Just Shut Up *85*

IV.   **FREEDOM & RESPONSIBILITY** *87*
        In and Out of the Trap *89*
        Turn Around *91*
        The Magic Bullet *94*
        Eat Your Lunch *96*
        A No-Win Situation *99*
        Aha *101*
        On Falling from Grace *104*
        The Gnawing *107*

V.   GRATITUDE & KINDNESS   *111*
Center Stage   *113*
Water, Water Everywhere   *115*
1944   *117*
Johnny B. Goode   *119*
I'll Never Leave You   *122*
If You Want to Be Happy
   for the Rest of Your Life   *124*
A Rainy Day   *127*
What Are You Waiting For?   *129*
Coffee with Milk   *131*

VI.   FAITH & MYSTERY   *135*
Would You Like Fries with That?   *137*
Chopsticks   *141*
Because I Can't   *143*
Uzbekistan   *147*
The GAIA Hypothesis   *150*
A Dime Store Mystery   *154*

VII.   TAKE IT ALL IN   *157*
Building Rome   *159*
Delaying Gratification   *162*
Jibber Jabber   *164*
Don't Do Something, Just Sit There   *166*
Take It All In   *168*
Faster Horses   *170*

VIII.   FEAR, COURAGE, & RESILIENCY   *173*
The Nature of the Beast   *175*
The Millrose Games   *177*

Just Another Day at the Ranch   *180*
Beauty and the Beast   *183*
Just Say No   *185*
Who's Running the Show?   *188*
Nausea   *191*
The Old Woman of the Seals   *195*
Over the Wall   *197*

IX.   AGING & DEATH   *201*
Grin and Bear It   *203*
The Bagel Store   *205*
Thinking About That Bagel Store   *207*
The End of the World   *209*
Face to Face   *213*
If I Only Knew Then What I
 Know Now   *216*
The Last Lecture   *218*
Would You Like Botox with That?   *223*

**X.   SHOWING UP FOR YOUR OWN
LIFE**   *227*
Go for It   *229*
Still Baking After All These Years   *232*
Don't Just Sit There, Do Something   *234*
Trust Me on This One   *235*
All Alone   *240*
Acceptance   *242*
It Is What It Is   *245*
What If It Is?   *248*
Curious George   *250*

Extraordinary with or Without
 the Extra   254
It's All Part of the Dance   257

Appendix A: Positive Psych 101   261
Epilogue   271
References   275

ACKNOWLEDGMENTS

Whenever possible, I have acknowledged the authors and storytellers responsible for the material in this book. The book does contain folk tales, quotes, and anecdotes of which I am unaware of any particular person being connected to. If I have failed to give an attribution when one was called for, I apologize, and future editions of this book will reflect appropriate acknowledgments.

Of course, I am thankful for the help and support from my wife, children, siblings, friends, colleagues, readers, and patients. Special thanks to Michael Pearson, Senior Editor at Goodman Beck Publishing, for his valuable editing and suggestions.

PREFACE

There is no certainty.
There is only adventure.
Even stars explode.
–Robert Assagioli

You are a story. If you don't like your story, you better start rewriting it now. You don't want your not liking your story to be a central part of your story. Life presses hard against us and takes a toll. We are all marked. No one escapes problems, shame, guilt, losses, deaths, and disappointments. Life happens and imprints deeply upon our psyche, soma, and spirit. Robert Holden's words are to the point:

> The truth is, you can walk up to anyone,
> on any street, in any city, in any country,
> in any culture, and on any continent, and
> if you say, "I'm so sorry to hear about

your problem," their reply to you will most likely be, "Who told you?!" Unhappiness isn't so special! It doesn't make you unique—lonely, maybe, but not unique. We all know what pain is. We've all "suffered," and we're all ready to heal... aren't we?

Writing in the *American Psychologist*, Laura King and Joshua Hicks discuss the importance of our being able to let go of "what might have been." We need to disengage from our past losses and lost opportunities and commit passionately to current projects, goals, and relationships that are in the service of our most deeply held values. The pain we feel is in the holding on. Healing is mostly about letting go. Freedom is found when we choose to move on. Despite our being marked by life, we need to develop the wherewithal and capacity to see the silver lining. That is not being pollyanish. It is instead, cultivating a hallmark trait of maturity. Also, when we understand that there are no guarantees and have the grace to live the life we have been given with courage, enthusiasm, and gratitude, we can garner the strength, resiliency, and wisdom to meet life's challenges as they press upon us. An African proverb tells us, "However long the night, the dawn will break."

The happy, complex person's palette is one that contains a rich array of color, and the mature artist, though genuinely marked by life, maintains an enthusiasm to put paint to the canvas of life in remarkable ways.

–Laura King and Joshua Hicks

And those who were seen dancing
were thought insane by those
who could not hear the music.
-Friedrich Nietzsche

INTRODUCTION

When we talk about settling
the world's problems, we're
barking up the wrong tree.

The world is perfect. It's a mess.
It has always been a mess.
We are not going to change it.

Our job is to straighten out our own lives.

–Joseph Campbell

Problems began in the Garden of Eden. It's true. There's always been trouble in paradise. Even in Genesis, there was war, evil, plagues, revenge, blame, and a vast variety of other difficulties. More recently, we've had Vietnam, tsunamis, genocide, 9/11, Iraq, global warming, voting in Florida, an economic depression, and more and more people struggling with unhappiness, anxiety, anger, frustration, substance abuse, addiction, and self-esteem and relationship problems.

Life is sometimes very difficult, and at times, the world seems upside down. Coping is essential, but it's vital to go way beyond that. The challenge is to find happiness, purpose, and meaning in the midst of where we find ourselves. Jose Ortega y Gasset has said, "We cannot put off living until we are ready. The most salient characteristic of life is its urgency, 'here and now' without any possible postponement. Life is fired at us point-blank."

Do we really need another book on happiness? Afterall, since I've written *The Happiness Solution*, another hundred books have addressed the same topic. Let me tell you why I decided to write another book on removing obstacles to your happiness. The "black dog" (depression) that Churchill experienced and wrote about is omnipresent. It nips at your heels, growls to frighten and discourage you, and its bark and its bite range from dispiriting to devastating.

Some people are somewhat unhappy. Others are in full-fledged despair. Unhappiness and depression are much more than a simple lowering of mood or feeling blue. Other signs can include a feeling of dissatisfaction or an "Is that all there is?" sense of the world. Being impatient, intolerant, critical, highly judgmental, and struggling with substances—food, alcohol, drugs—can all be connected to even mild depression. So can a sleep disturbance, poor memory, and difficulty concentrating. And, of course, feelings of helplessness, hopelessness, or worthlessness are usually lurking nearby. Physical illnesses, aging, and losing your way spiritually may also be involved.

The World Health Organization estimates that depression is the fourth most debilitating disease in the world. By 2020, it will be the second biggest. Almost 50 percent of the world's population will, at some point in their lives, struggle mightily with depression. The 11th leading cause of death in the United States is suicide. Approximately every 39 seconds, someone in the U.S. is trying to kill themselves. That translates to thousands of people a day. And those are only the people we find out about. There are roughly 25 attempts for every person who actually kills himself. So it turns out that every 16 minutes, a successful suicide (if you could call it that) happens. Around the clock. Twenty-four seven, to use an expression I thought I would never use.

Rates of depression and anxiety are on the rise. If you run out of your Paxil, just shout out at the supermarket, "Does anyone here have some Paxil?" A line will begin to form. The same can be said for Prozac, Zoloft, Lexapro, Ativan, Xanax, and other psychotropic medications.

All of this suggests that life can be quite harrowing. I think it was the noted psychiatrist Harry Stack Sullivan who said something to the effect that:

> The question isn't why do people kill themselves, but rather, why doesn't everyone kill themselves?

Part of our predicament is that we have to find happiness, joy, purpose, and meaning in life while we are aware of our impending plight—that we and everyone we love are dying. This death-consciousness or denial of it can and does contribute mightily to our unhappiness. I think this is our main challenge in life—to learn to deal with the certainty of our deaths in such a way that our lives are not diminished. Steinbeck said, "A sad soul can kill you far quicker than a germ."

This book is about how to coexist with the upside down world and acquire the wisdom to appreciate the paradox that the world is fine *as is*. This book is about learning how to get out of your own way and how not to create obstacles that interfere with your happiness. It's about learning what to think about and what to let go of. It's about focusing on the here and now. It's about finding out what your strengths are and utilizing them daily. It's positive psychology, Zen wisdom, cognitive behavioral therapy, and showing up for and taking responsibility for your own life. Ultimately, it's about finding joy, purpose, and meaning.

May your life be long and happy.

HOW HAPPY ARE YOU?

Please read each of the following group of statements and select the one statement in each group that best describes the way you have been feeling for the past week, including today.

1.   (a)   I feel miserable almost all the time.
        (b)   I often feel miserable.
        (c)   I usually feel neutral.
        (d)   I usually feel pretty good.
        (e)   I feel great almost all the time.

2.   (a)   I find life to be boring all the time.
        (b)   I'm pretty bored with most aspects of life.
        (c)   I find life boring at times, but at other times, it interests me.
        (d)   I'm interested in most aspects of life.
        (e)   I find life and living to be absolutely fascinating.

3. (a)   I have no direction or life purpose.
    (b)   I'm unsure about my life direction and purpose.
    (c)   Sometimes I feel like I know my life purpose.
    (d)   I'm pretty clear about my life purpose and direction.
    (e)   My life purpose and direction is crystal clear.

4. (a)   I have no energy and feel tired almost all the time.
    (b)   I often feel tired and lethargic.
    (c)   I usually have enough energy to do what I need to do.
    (d)   Most of the time I feel energetic and enthusiastic.
    (e)   I'm bursting with energy and enthusiasm almost all the time.

5. (a)   I'm extremely pessimistic about the future.
    (b)   There are times when I feel pessimistic about the future.
    (c)   I'm not sure about the future, one way or the other.
    (d)   I'm pretty optimistic about the future.
    (e)   I'm extremely optimistic and excited about the future.

6. (a)   I don't have any close friends.
    (b)   I have a few friends, but none I really consider close.
    (c)   I have a few good friends and family members with whom I'm close.

(d) I have quite a few good friends.

(e) I have lots of good friends and feel I easily connect with everyone.

7. (a) I don't think I have any strengths at all.

(b) I'm not sure whether or not I have any strengths.

(c) I'm getting to know my strengths.

(d) I know my strengths and try to use them when I can.

(e) I know exactly what my strengths are and I use them all the time.

8. (a) I never enjoy myself no matter what I'm doing.

(b) I find it difficult to enjoy life in the moment.

(c) I try to enjoy life as much as I can.

(d) I enjoy myself most of the time.

(e) I thoroughly enjoy every moment.

9. (a) I have absolutely nothing for which to be grateful.

(b) There's not much in my life for which I'm grateful.

(c) I'm grateful for a few things in my life.

(d) I have quite a few things in my life for which I'm grateful.

(e) I'm extremely grateful for so many things in my life.

10. (a) I've accomplished nothing.

(b)   I've not accomplished much in life.

(c)   I've accomplished about as much as the average person.

(d)   I've accomplished more in life than most people.

(e)   I've accomplished a great deal more in life than most people.

Score each question from 1 to 5 where (a) equals 1 and (e) equals 5 (your maximum score, therefore, should be 50).

If you scored 40 or above, you're doing extremely well. Keep up the great work.

If you scored 30-39, you're doing pretty well but might like to review the questions on which you scored 3 or below and consider how you might improve in these areas.

If you scored below 29, you could be much happier!

Reprinted with permission of thehappinessinstitute.com.

IT'S ALL PART OF THE DANCE

Finding Happiness in an Upside Down World

The Stories

If you can talk, you can sing.
If you can walk, you can dance.
–Zimbabwean Proverb

I.
ATTITUDE

Dancing in all its forms cannot be
excluded from the curriculum of all noble
education; dancing with the feet, with ideas,
with words, and, need I add that one must
be able to dance with the pen?
–Friedrich Nietzsche

MY FIRST TICONDEROGA

All of my friends and colleagues tell me I should use the computer to write my books. They rave about the ease of shifting paragraphs around and so on. I tell them that I write my books using pads and pencils. They shake their collective heads in dismay. I guess I'm a dinosaur. So be it.

I'm just not a high tech kind of guy. Maybe I'm a bit slow to jump on the latest and greatest. My wife and children will tell you that I'm very low maintenance. I don't know the names of clothing designers. I have no idea what the hot cars are, and 60-inch TV screens don't interest me. I think the way I write my books reflects me and my values. I use extra-thick yellow pencils with big erasers. I guess these pencils are made especially for little kids. On each pencil are the words "My First Ticonderoga."

The pencil erasers get quite a workout. The eraser and the pencil seem to be used up about the same time. Depending on my mood, sometimes I'll just cross out words or paragraphs rather than erase them. Sometimes, halfway through a story, I'll crumple up the paper and start all over. I try to write stories that let you know who I am and what I believe in. My main goal is to have each story help you in some way. This story, about a low-tech guy who writes books on pads using kids' extra-thick pencils with huge erasers, is really about the following:

–Making mistakes is inevitable, unless you're dead.

–Give yourself permission to erase, without feeling like you failed.

–It's fine to reevaluate.

–Have goals and work toward them passionately.

–Trust yourself.

–Sometimes, your way may be fine for you even if it's not the newest and most improved version available.

–Don't give yourself a hard time.

It's quite possible that after reading this story, you'll think I'm a lousy dresser who's behind the times and is too lazy to learn a word processing program that would make his writing a lot easier. But since I don't give myself a hard time and always give myself the benefit of the doubt, I'll go with a different conclusion—I like writing in the great outdoors with my 8x11 pad and my first Ticonderoga.

LIFE IS BIZARRE

It's true. We all shake our heads from time to time when certain events occur. The old cliché is correct — truth is stranger than fiction. Things happen that seem virtually unbelievable. Ask people to tell you the weirdest things that ever happened to them. Everyone's got a tale that reflects just how bizarre life is. I've got a few.

The world is not necessarily fair or just. Things happen. Even religious people sometimes get the feeling that no one is watching the store. If you expect an orderly world that makes sense all of the time, you're being quite naïve. Things will happen that have no logical explanation. Paranormal happenings abound. The last few books I've written have subtitles indicating that the world, at times, seems upside down. We have genocide and miracles. Priests and rabbis molest children. Good Samaritans give up their lives for total strangers. Really, are you surprised by anything?

After one look at this planet,
any visitor from outer space would
say, "I want to see the manager."
–William S. Burroughs

Any measure of peace of mind and security you may attain will be directly connected to your acceptance of change and the strangeness of life. If your happiness depends on life being predictable or fair, you're in trouble.

Of course life is bizarre:
the more bizarre it gets,
the more interesting it is.
The only way to approach it
is to make yourself some popcorn
and enjoy the show.
–Anonymous

20,000 MOMENTS

Princeton professor and Nobel Prize-winning scientist Daniel Kahneman has said that each day we experience approximately 20,000 moments. Each moment is defined as a few seconds long and has the potential to be experienced in a myriad of ways. Unfortunately, we take most of these moments for granted. We typically don't consider the potential impact of our choices in defining the quality of our moments. For example, if you encounter a person, you can influence what a moment feels like, depending on whether you decide to:

-smile
-frown
-ignore the person
-acknowledge the person by name
-give a compliment
-say something critical

The Broadway musical *Rent* began on a side street in New York City. It wasn't even considered Off-Broadway. The overwhelming majority of these Off-Off-Broadway shows have little chance of big time success. But people were deeply touched by the show and word quickly spread. Not only did this rock musical make it to Broadway, it won the Tony and Pulitzer Prize. It was based on Puccini's 1896 opera *La Boheme* and celebrated the zest, courage, and hope of artists and rebels.

The play opened one hundred years after *La Boheme* and was written by the bohemian writer Jonathan Larson. The author wrote from the heart and tragically died in his twenties on the day of its final dress rehearsal, just before opening night. The show's most magical moments come in an unforgettable song called "Seasons of Love." Here are some of the lyrics:

five hundred twenty-five thousand six hundred minutes
five hundred twenty-five thousand moments so dear
five hundred twenty-five thousand six hundred minutes
how do you measure, measure a year?

in daylights
in sunsets
in midnights
in cups of coffee
in inches, in miles, in laughter, in strife

in five hundred twenty-five thousand six hundred minutes
how do you measure a year in a life?

how about love?
how about love?

how about love?
measure in love ...
seasons of love ...
seasons of love ...

Life is a series of moments. You can go through them on automatic pilot or you can experience them with your eyes and ears wide open. You have a choice whether to embrace the moment consciously and vitally or whether to approach it half-baked or half-heartedly. Twenty thousand moments a day to empower yourself and your life or to choose passivity, pessimism, boredom, and lethargy. Twenty thousand moments each day. Phew! That's a lot of responsibility. That's a lot of freedom. Are you up to it? I hope so. Your happiness depends on it.

MAX'S SANDWICH SHOP

There has been a lot of fuss lately about the "Law of Attraction." A book and video called *The Secret* made it to Oprah, and the rush was on to discover the latest key to the universe. As it turns out, *The Secret* wasn't really much of a secret. It was based on the aforementioned law of attraction, which has been around in some way, shape, or form for centuries. The essence of it is that people experience physical and mental manifestations that correspond to their predominant thoughts, feelings, and actions. What you think, believe, and feel attract and produce related positive or negative experiences.

In other words, the law of attraction states that, to a large degree, you get what you think about. Your thoughts determine your experience. In essence, you create much of your own world. According to quantum physics, thoughts have energy that attracts similar energy. So, the idea is that if you know what you want and ask the universe (God, nature, the Force, etc.) for it, and you focus enthusiastically on this, and you feel and behave as if you've already acquired it, and you're open to receiving it gracefully and gratefully, you'll get it.

All that being said, I don't believe it. Yes, certainly to a degree, it's true. But overall, it's too naïve and simplistic. What I do believe is that we do have tremendous power and influence over how we feel and whether we are ultimately happy and successful. Our thoughts, expectations, and beliefs are crucial with regard to the quality of our lives, but they don't guarantee that you'll get all you want and won't get what you don't want.

In *Zen and the Art of Happiness*, Chris Prentiss tells the story of Max's Sandwich Shop:

Max owned a thriving sandwich shop. There were almost always people waiting in line to eat at his little shop. He gave away free pickles, free potato chips, sometimes a free soft drink, and his sandwiches were famous for being overstuffed.

One day his son, who lived in a distant city, came to visit. They had a good visit, but as the son was leaving, he told his father, "Since I've been here, I've been observing how you run the sandwich shop, and I have to tell you for your own good that you're making a big mistake giving away all those extras. The country's economy is in bad shape. People are out of work, and they have less money to spend. If you don't cut back on the free items and on your portion sizes, you'll be in a bad way before long too." His father was amazed, thanked his son, and told him he would consider it all.

After his son left, Max followed his advice. He stopped giving away free items and he cut back on the generous portions of food in his sandwiches. Before long, after many disappointed customers had stopped coming, he wrote his son: "You were right! The country's economy is in bad shape, and I'm experiencing the results of it right here in my sandwich shop!"

PUTTING IT IN PERSPECTIVE

I ran a mile at the local high school track. I had hoped to run it in 6 minutes and 40 seconds. Checking my stopwatch, I was disappointed to see my time of 6 minutes and 47 seconds. I shook my head back and forth to indicate mild disgust with myself and wondered why my time was slow. At that moment, I noticed a girl approaching the track with her mother. She appeared to be about 18 years old and was dressed very nicely. I believe she had cerebral palsy. As her mother held her hand, she made her way around the track, inches at a time. Each step was an effort of will. Grunting and drooling, she made her way around the entire track with her mother's continual encouragement. It took her a very long time to do this, but I waited until she finished. I felt a bit ashamed that I had been so concerned and upset about my time in the mile. I tried to get perspective on life in general and myself and my *problems* in particular.

It's been said that there's no worse toothache than your own.

I think everyone should take time to spend a day walking around the Sloane Kettering Cancer Hospital in New York or a similar facility. To put it mildly, it's a very sobering experience. The sights and sounds you witness may help you gain perspective on the problems you are dealing with. It may not be a fun-filled afternoon for you, but it may certainly be eye-opening and worthwhile.

Once a year, my wife and I and our children volunteer to help at the Special Olympics Summer Games. We serve as track escorts, which means we help Special Olympians to the starting line of events they are participating in. These athletes are dealing with day-to-day mental and physical challenges that most people never have to grapple with. Their grit, courage, and determination is enormous. Their spirit is contagious.

It always helps me to put things in context and reach different conclusions. For example, to realize how trivial it is that I ran a 6:47 mile when I was shooting for a 6:40. When I'm too absorbed with myself or engaging in unnecessary self-scrutinization, I try to switch from the zoom lens to a wide angle lens that allows me to view the bigger picture and see what I was looking at from a totally different perspective. It usually helps a great deal. Try it. Stop zooming in on your problems and put on the wide angle lens. Changing lenses can be an eye-opening experience.

NEVER SAY NEVER

The novice monk asked the Zen Master, "What is the heart of teaching?"

The venerable old sage replied, "It's fifty percent encouragement."

"Oh," said the monk. "What's the other fifty percent?"

The master replied, "Encouragement."

To feel discouraged at times is natural. After all, as I've said in many of my stories, life is hard. It's filled with things that don't happen the way we'd like them to happen. We always have to adapt to and deal with changes in our lives while we yearn for security and stability. Of course we'll get discouraged from time to time.

I think the common denominator to most emotional problems is a strong or chronic sense of discouragement. At my office, I have seen thousands of people who struggle with anxiety, panic, phobias, obsessive-compulsive disorders, depression, bi-polar disorder, marital or job-related issues, family problems, grieving, and post-traumatic stress disorders, just to name a few. They are discouraged. They get stuck in their discouragement. My job is to do everything I can to help them get unstuck and feel better.

I tell them, "Don't think that the way you feel now is the way you're always going to feel." Discouragement brings with it a myopic tunnel or funnel-like vision. I remind them that change is a certainty. Some people find that comforting; others find it frightening. We work on getting them to think differently and behave differently. If they do that, the feelings will come along for the ride. We don't want instant replay. If they're very discouraged and don't change their thoughts and behaviors, they'll just get the same day again and again. Groundhog Day! (I'm assuming you've seen the movie. If not, it's worth the rental.)

If you are stuck in a place where you're very discouraged, my advice to you is a bit paradoxical:

–Wait. This too shall pass.

–Do something. Think and behave differently.
We're not interested in the status quo.

Keep in mind how resilient you are and keep going in the direction that is meaningful for you.

In 1898, young Albert Einstein applied for admission to the Munich Technical Institute — and was turned down. The reason?

The young man, the Institute declared, "showed no promise" as a student. By 1905, he had formulated his special theory of relativity.

HOW DO I LOVE THEE?

Eos, the Greek goddess of the dawn, had an unquenchable appetite for handsome young men. This plight stemmed from her upsetting Aphrodite, the goddess of Love. Although Eos had made love to the gods, she was forced to make do with mortal men. She kidnapped the beautiful Trojan youths Ganymede and Tithonus to be her lovers. Zeus fancied Ganymede and stole him to be his cup-bearer. Zeus appeased the angry Eos by granting her one wish of her choosing. She asked for immortality for her lover, Tithonus. What she neglected to do was to ask for eternal youth for him. Indeed, Tithonus lived forever, but became weak and racked with pain as his youth and attractiveness withered away.

The single biggest problem in
communication is the illusion
that it has taken place.
–George Bernard Shaw

Eos grew intolerant and felt repulsed by the aging Tithonus. She locked him in a room to get old by himself. (There was no "for better or for worse.") Despite begging for death, Tithonus had eternal life. Eos was also dissatisfied, and her tears are said to be the morning dew.

Relationships can be very disappointing. Sure, they start out well enough — maybe even better than that. Sometimes, it's love at first sight or first this or first that. Eros, the god of erotic love, captures us. We feel the chemistry. We idealize our partners. There are very few experiences that compare favorably to romantic love in bloom.

As relationships evolve, a major obstacle presents itself. That obstacle is called reality. Our fantasies about what our lives with our partners would be like or should be like are punctured. Realities involving doing the dishes, paying the mortgage, and changing diapers are but a few examples of what erodes Eros. We become disheartened and disenchanted. "He's not the man (woman) I married," is a classic refrain. Disappointment reigns supreme as one or both partners feel neglected, unappreciated, angry, or hurt. As years go by, aging changes faces and bodies and presents new challenges to relationships. Many couples are not up to the task. Dr. Michael Vincent Miller has written eloquently about these issues:

> The challenge is how to live a good life in spite of disappointment. Among the least promising ways is to blame others. Partners, who blame each other for what goes wrong in a relationship, wind up acting like people pushing past each other to get on a crowded subway or bus, one

saying, "I'm late!" and the other replying,
"No, I'm late!"

Dr. Miller makes the critical point that people need to move beyond the blame game and transform their disappointment in a relationship into something livable, viable, and useful for each person. I think this is part of the maturation process. We have to learn that it's alright for us not to get everything we want in life and in relationships. I'm not advocating staying in poor or destructive relationships. This is not a grin-and-bare-it philosophy. It's about each person developing empathy for the other's predicament. It's about a shared sense of responsibility and commitment to find ways to make the relationship better. It's not about finger pointing and name calling. It's about both people looking at themselves and recognizing their own roles in helping to create the relationship they are not thrilled with. To be disappointed in love is less the issue than what you do with that disappointment.

The first drafts of love are usually
in need of considerable revision.
–Michael Vincent Miller

MY BROTHER-IN-LAW

I'd like to tell you a story I heard a long time ago. When his father was upset with him for doing so much charitable work, Ram Dass reminded him of work that he (the father) had done for free. Ram Dass queried as to why the father hadn't issued a charge for his services. His father said, "Of course I'm not going to charge him. He's my brother-in-law." To which Ram Dass replied, "Well, that's my predicament. Everyone's my brother-in-law."

In a very real sense, the world has become your neighborhood. The population has greatly increased, but the world isn't as big as it used to be. Generations of mathematicians, sociologists, and physicists have been consumed with the ideas of network theory. Frigyes Karinthy, a Hungarian author, published a 1929 short story called "Chains" that was brilliant in its recognition of our "shrinking world." Karinthy believed that the growing density of human networks and technological breakthroughs in communication and travel made the social distance between people smaller. Friendship networks spanned greater distances than ever and connected people all over the globe. In "Chains," Karinthy's characters believed that any two individuals could be connected through networking a maximum of five acquaintances.

Almost 40 years later, Stanley Milgram, a Harvard professor and extraordinary researcher in experimental social psychology, conducted a number of studies to investigate this phenomenon. Miligram's carefully designed research concluded that people seemed to be connected by, on average, approximately six friendship links. In 1990, an American writer named John Guare penned *Six Degrees of Separation*, which later became a movie and was responsible for the phrase "six degrees of separation" becoming a part of everyday vernacular. So, if a person is one step away from each person she knows and two steps away from each person who is known by one of the people she knows, then everyone is no more than six steps away from any person on the planet.

In some strange way, I derive a measure of comfort from this connectedness. At the very least, I find it curious and interesting. It validates my sense that we're all somewhat related and that we're all more alike than different. It also strikes me as being very human, spiritual, and hope-inspiring. I also find it fun and playful to think of the possible networks that connect me to a farmer in Nebraska, the Dalai Lama, a teacher in Zimbabwe, a serial killer in Oklahoma, and an American Indian elder on the reservation outside of Santa Fe. It's a small world after all!

A DIFFERENT BALL GAME

A number of my friends have retired. We're of that age. I'm not interested. I've worked forever. Maybe even longer than that. My parents owned a struggling neighborhood candy store. It opened 6 in the morning and closed 10 at night, 7 days a week. That's when penny candy really sold for a penny.

We were relatively poor. I only had one stripe on my pajamas. (That's a joke. Admittedly, a bad one.) We lived in a dingy flat above the store. Frequently, the electric company would turn off our service and the telephone company would shut down our party line phone. Not being able to meet our bills, public agencies would post notices on all the local telephone poles announcing a public auction of our furniture and possessions. We had to park our 1948 Buick blocks away from our home so it wouldn't be repossessed. Getting the picture? If not, picture shame, embarrassment, and frustration in a dysfunctional but loving family with a good work ethic.

I always loved being in the store. It was where I saw family and friends and learned the importance of hard work. As a child, I worked in other arenas to make my own money. I shined shoes, sold salve door to door, carried people's grocery bags, shoveled snow, collected old bottles, newspapers, and rags to sell, and so on. All this was while I was in elementary school.

I continued working all through school. Between working, college loans, and eventually the G.I. bill, I was able to attend five colleges without ever taking a nickel from my parents. Working has always been important to me. I value it highly and am thankful I'm able to work full-time. In case you're wondering, I'm not a workaholic. Not even close. I treat myself well and with respect. Being productive through work is part of what produces happiness for me.

I'm concerned about the children growing up today. They get trophies just for showing up. They're coddled, over-protected, and are generally not given enough responsibilities. At an early age, they're given a plethora of gadgetry — including cell phones, computers, and the latest video game systems. Many of these kids are growing up with an egocentric attitude and a less than stellar work ethic. The dream of many teenagers and young adults is to make a lot of money quickly and retire young so they can continue to indulge their appetite for play. They don't value work in and of itself but see it as a means to get more playtime. When they get into the world of work, it can be a bit of a rude awakening. They don't get trophies for just showing up. It's a different ball game. As the overworked expression goes, "Welcome to the real world."

> How painful to see people
> all wrapped up in themselves.
> –Ryokan

At least for me, valuing work, enjoying it, and looking forward to working for years to come adds to my contentment. I like the idea of earning what I get and feeling humility rather than entitlement. Yes, I grew up poor, never lived in a house, was expected to work diligently at an early age, and never got a trophy for just showing up—and I feel pretty darn good about it.

THE HUMBLE DOG

In Greek mythology, there is the story of Daedalus and his son, Icarus. They were imprisoned inside a huge labyrinth. The resourceful father was able to make each of them a pair of wings. So it was that they were able to escape. They were free. Knowing the risks and responsibilities that come along with freedom, Daedalus warned his son, "Don't fly too high or the sun will melt the wax on your wings and you will fall." Icarus was young and lacked his father's wisdom. He felt such exhilaration as he flew, he forgot to heed his father's warning. He flew much too high. When he got too close to the sun, the wax melted. Icarus fell into the sea and drowned.

I used to wear a t-shirt when I ran that had a picture of a huge dog and the imprint "If You Can't Run with the Big Dogs, Stay on the Porch." In retrospect, I was as brash and immature as Icarus. I'm a bit ashamed that I wore that shirt and I wouldn't consider wearing it again. I've lost a t-shirt but gained humility. The word "humble" comes from the Latin humus, which means "earth." Humility is derived from the Latin humilis, which means "on the ground." A humble person doesn't have his nose up in the air and does have his feet on the ground. He is of the world and not above the fray.

One of my running routes took me past a neighbor's house. Tom had little use of his legs because of a muscular disease. One day, as I ran past Tom's house, he waved me down to ask me a question. As we stood face to face, I realized I was wearing the Big Dogs t-shirt. After that day, I never wore that t-shirt again. It's never too late to call yourself on the carpet. I was arrogant. I'm not anymore. I'm luckier than Icarus. I didn't fall into the sea and drown.

Mary Oliver's poem "Long Afternoon at the Edge of Little Sister Pond" is one of my favorites. Its essence reflects numerous qualities associated with happiness, including humility, an appreciation of life's mysteries, and the awe connected to the universe:

> As for life,
> I'm humbled,
> I'm without words
> Sufficient to say
>
> how it has been hard as flint,
> and soft as a spring pond,
> both of these
> and over and over,

and long pale afternoons besides,
and so many mysteries
beautiful as eggs in a nest,
still unhatched

though warm and watched over
by something I have never seen –
a tree angel, perhaps,
or a ghost of holiness.

Every day I walk out into the world
to be dazzled, then to be reflective.

II.
CHOICES

Will you, won't you, will you,
won't you, will you join the dance?
–Lewis Carroll

ON LIVING IN POTEMKIN VILLAGE

In the 18th century, Grigori Aleksandrovich Potemkin had elaborate fake villages built in order to impress Catherine the Great on her tours of the Ukraine and the Crimea. So it was that the term "Potemkin Village" was born. It refers to an impressive facade or display that hides an undesirable fact or state. It is the equivalent of a false front.

One of the obstacles to happiness is rooted in the discrepancy between how you present yourself to the world and how you really feel about yourself. Many people believe that if others got to know them intimately, ultimately those others would be very surprised and disappointed. You would be taken aback by the percentage of people who feel like imposters. They feel as if they would never stand up to the scrutiny of careful assessment with respect to their being as loveable or worthwhile as they would like to be.

In other words, there is a large gap between the outer and

inner. They show the world a facade, perhaps a very impressive one indeed. But it is like an illusion. It is like building a Potemkin Village, hiding what they deem to be their undesirable traits or essences. This may be at least a part of the rush to own designer clothing, fancy cars, and the newest and best of everything. That is neither the antidote nor the answer to the question of "How can I be happier with myself and my life?"

I would invite you to work on narrowing the gap between who you think you are and who you would like to be. And, I have two words for you that can make all the difference: Start now! It is never too late to become the person you feel good about being. You don't need to impress Catherine the Great. You need only to practice cultivating characteristics and behaviors that continue to narrow the aforementioned gap. For example:

–If you believe you're selfish, practice generosity of spirit.
–If you believe you're angry, practice patience.
–If you believe you're uncaring, practice compassion.
–If you believe you know best, practice humility.
–If you believe you're rigid, practice flexibility.
–If you believe you're weak, practice assertiveness.
–If you believe you're critical, practice kindness.
–If you believe you're distant, practice loving.
–If you believe you're controlling, practice letting go.
–If you believe you're immoral, practice morality.
–If you believe you're hateful, practice forgiveness.

Develop your list of what creates the gap. What is the false front hiding that you wish wasn't there or don't want others to find out about? Figure out what you need to practice and begin now. Not being a Potemkin Village is part of achieving happiness. Don't be discouraged. Anyone who ever got to be who she wanted to be had to begin where she was. It will definitely be worth your while, most likely not only to you, but to others as well. Start now.

LET IT GO

There's something you're holding on to. It may be a fear or a feeling such as anger. Whatever it is, it's not in your best interest to hold on to it. Holding on creates a physiology of stress. Picture holding on to the edge of a cliff and how your body would react as you continued to hold on longer and longer. Or, picture holding up a pitcher of water with one arm. The longer that you hold on to it, the more tension and stress accumulate. Holding it up for 10 seconds is very different than holding it up for minutes or hours.

Holding on has its own unique biochemistry. In the animal kingdom, stress is dealt with by the classical fight-or-flight-or-freeze response. Animals attack or flee or become immobilized because of their fear. With humans, I propose a fourth "F" be added. When under stress, humans respond with fight-or-flight-or-freeze-or-fester. The holding on to is the festering. Holding on creates psychosomatic illnesses, real physical maladies that have psychological roots. This festering is the stuff that migraines, high blood pressure, anxiety, depression, and various gastrointestinal disturbances are made of—just to name a few.

The antidote to holding on to is to let it go. Learning to let go is an important principle of mental health. Whatever it is that you're holding on to is not worth it. It's too high a price to pay. Let it go and you'll start to create the physiology connected to relaxation. Whereas we had four "F" words connected to holding on, we have four "R" words related to letting it go:

-Release
-Relax
-Restore
-Regenerate

Letting it go leads to the release of the pent up emotions, which will help you to move into being more relaxed—which will restore your energy and equilibrium, enabling you to regenerate and feel markedly better. The suffering comes from holding on. The solution comes when you let go. Let it go and give yourself the freedom to be happier.

A HISTORY LESSON

It was a majestic looking pond with the shimmering sun alighting upon the deep blue-green water. Clean, crisp, and beautiful. After many years, a prolonged drought lowered the water level of the pond to the point where many items that were unseen now became visible. Discarded spare tires, an old rusty bike, beer bottles, soda cans, a black high top sneaker, garbage, and all sorts of objects in various states of disrepair and decomposition. It was all beneath the surface, unseen. But it was ready to surface given the right conditions, or rather, given the wrong conditions.

Each of us is like that pond. We all have demons lurking. If we have histories, we have demons. If we are alive, we have demons. I don't think anyone is immune. All of our most horrible fears and fantasies and our most terrible deeds go into our daimonic. Everything that we ever did or thought that we were ashamed of or embarrassed about enters our daimonic. Intense feelings of guilt, hostility, and unacceptable sexuality may also be part of it. The daimonic is part and parcel of the human experience and resides below the surface, littering our ponds. Denial or repression leads to leakage or eruption, which produces distress and symptoms.

People eventually trust me enough to share their demons with me. Many patients say, "I never told this to anyone, but …." I am like an exorcist and people deposit their demons with me, which leads to them having freed up energy for day-to-day living and much more peace of mind. Harboring their secrets was the cause of much of their distress. They come to understand that the beautiful, sunlit shimmering pond is only part of the story. Underneath the surface is our history.

We all are unique. Similar, but different. We've all had childhoods. Sometimes, it's the luck of the draw. Some of us have had very loving parents and some of us haven't. Some of us have been surrounded by warmth and praise and encouragement. Others have been immersed in rejection, apathy, and criticism. We've all experienced adolescence and its nightmares. Some of us have been abused in one or more ways. Yes, there's no getting around it. We all have histories, some better than others.

As a psychologist, I get to hear a lot of histories. Nothing surprises me. There's a lot of pain out there. Many people feel damaged in significant ways. That's understandable. They have had psychologically devastating experiences. After major traumas, just like with natural disasters, there's an aftermath that needs to be dealt with. We can't change history. The events have taken place. All we can do is try to clean up, restore some sense of order, take stock of the damage, feel our pain, and learn what we need to do to feel better and live our lives well.

If your history has impacted upon you in such a way that it diminishes your self-esteem or interferes with your productivity, relationships, or happiness, listen carefully. You need to set yourself free. If your history contains the chains that bind you, you're stuck in a discouraging life situation. Here's the key to your freedom:

> You can't change history,
> but you can reinterpret it.

For example, let's suppose that your father was cruel-hearted, critical, and continually found fault with you. You may feel that your suffering at his hands has produced your lack of confidence, mistrust in men, and depressive tendencies. That is a main theme in your story. "I'm damaged. My father hated me. I'll never forgive him. There's something terribly wrong with me." There is another way to look at it. How about this? "My father was just a fallible human being who had a difficult childhood himself. He used bad judgment and wasn't loving, but not only did I survive his wrath, it proved my strength and resiliency. Not all men are like my father. Letting go of my disappointment, hurt, and anger is something I can get better at."

We haven't changed history, but we've reinterpreted it to set you free. This is called reframing. You are not lying to yourself about what happened, but you're seeing it through a different lens. You're coming at it from a different angle. In a notebook of mine, I found the following explanation of reframing, but no citation as to its origin:

> The technique of reframing capitalizes on the
> subjective nature of personal stories to un-

cover underlying, underemphasized themes in people's stories that are potentially helpful. Its purpose is to arrive at an authentic and helpful story, one that does not eliminate the pain that hardship can cause but that also includes the strength that is forged in the struggle to prevail.

Reinterpreting history can turn your life storyline from a destructive one to a constructive one. For example, instead of having a theme of failure and not being good enough as the basis of your story, you can substitute the themes of determination, perseverance, and adequacy.

What do you need to reframe? Start now. Today will be history tomorrow. What's holding you back? What's interfering with your happiness? Get out those old history lessons. Think about them differently. Look at them under a different light. See anything from a new perspective? What else can you tell yourself about that history? You're never too old to learn something new.

The truth is that our finest moments are most likely to occur when we are feeling deeply uncomfortable, unhappy, or unfulfilled. For it is only in such moments, propelled by our discomfort, that we are likely to step out of our ruts and start searching for different ways or truer answers.

–M. Scott Peck

THE STOCK EXCHANGE

I'd like you to take a look at your life. Take inventory. How do you feel about the following?

- How much time do you spend alone? Is it enough, too much, or not enough?

- How much time do you spend with your family? Enough, too much, or not enough?

- What about alone time with just your significant other? Not enough? Too much? Just right? And, how much time do you and your significant other spend socializing with others? Enough?

- How about time spent working?

- How much time do you spend on hobbies or pleasurable activities?

–What about time spent on the computer? Are you addicted?

–How much television do you watch? Be honest. Most people underestimate.

–Do you spend any time volunteering? Is it enough, too much, or not enough?

–How much time do you spend exercising? Not enough, enough, or too much?

–How much time do you spend with friends?

–How much sleep do you get?

–Do you spend time on satisfying religious or spiritual leanings? If so, is it enough or not enough?

I could go on and on with this, but I think you get the idea of what I mean when I ask you to take stock of your life. The reason I refer to this story as "The Stock Exchange" is this: After your inventory reveals what you have too much of, you can exchange it for what you don't have enough of. You'll be able to come up with a different formula regarding how you spend your time hour to hour, day to day, week to week, and month to month. Hopefully this formula will be balanced enough to lead to increased joy and meaning for you.

Remember, everyone gets the same 24 hours that you do. It's the choices that you make on how to spend your time today that create happiness or sadness. It's the choices that you make today that shape your life and take it in certain directions. Take inventory. Do it today.

SAY WHAT?

Many years ago, two anthropologists—Edward Sapir and Benjamin Whorf—came up with the hypothesis of linguistic relativism. This postulates that the language we use affects how we view and experience the world. For example, in George Orwell's novel *1984*, he suggests that if a particular culture doesn't have the vocabulary to express the ideas underlying a revolution, they will not be able to revolt. The Sapir-Whorf hypothesis claims that your language and the words you choose determine the way you will interpret the world around you. Your words produce thoughts that create your feelings, which, in turn, influence your behaviors.

Tell me how you feel when you read the following:

Exciting * Fun * Laughter * Love * Peace *
Possibility * Joy * Beauty * Alive * Great

How do you feel? Now, read the next group of words:

Sadness * Boredom * Apathy * Hate *
War * Stagnation * Despair *
Depression * Anger * Death

Well, how do you feel? Did you notice any differences? Read the paragraphs below and see if you notice a difference in how you feel after the first paragraph versus the second paragraph.

When I think about the future, I become energized. There is so much I can accomplish. Life is good. I have so much to look forward to. Life is full of possibilities and I have been blessed.

or

When I think about the future, I become despairing. There is nothing to look forward to. Life is terrible. I feel miserable and always will be. I feel hopeless and cursed.

This is more than semantics. The language that you use is very powerful. It creates your reality. It alters your perceptions and confirms your expectations. How you feel about yourself, others, and life is greatly influenced by the language that you use in that almost nonstop conversation that's going on in your head. We all know that words can greatly harm someone when verbal abuse is at play. That's obvious because it is a blatant example of what happens at one end of the verbal continuum. But there are less obvious damaging labels and words being used regularly that have a great negative impact. The more subtle the counterproductive language you use is, and the more negative nuances there are, the more verbal and emotional abuse you inflict on yourself.

To be happier, try to tune in to the words you use that diminish you and others—the words that create self-doubt, low self-esteem, lack of confidence, fatigue, discouragement, pessimism, and so on. Those words have that destructive power that insures a status quo of being less than happy and unfulfilled.

Make an effort to develop a different vocabulary—one that nourishes rather than malnourishes. If it helps, write out a list of such words that you want to incorporate into how you see yourself and your world. Study them, just like the weekly vocabulary words you'd study in grade school. Use them in your mind, in your thinking, in your speech, and let them begin to help you to produce different and better experiences for you.

It may be a myth, but remember how we were always taught that the Eskimos had 16 or more different words for snow? That supposedly enabled them to actually see snow differently than non-Eskimos. Their language created the ability to see things that others didn't. Language alters perception. You can experience the world differently by learning new language to frame how you see yourself, others, and life—the language of happiness.

TWO CENTS

Here's my two cents, even though you didn't ask for it: Eat your vegetables. Take your vitamins. Wear your seatbelt. Exercise. Don't smoke. Don't abuse food, alcohol, or people. Let go of anger. Be kind to animals. Help others. And, here's my answer as to why you should do all that: "Just for the health of it!"

You are the sum of your choices. If you value life and value yourself, the likelihood is that you'll make healthy choices, and that increases your chances of having a lengthier lifespan, more disability-free living, and more happiness. Studies have shown that people who don't wear their seatbelts are more likely to be smokers than those who wear them. The non-seatbelt users are less likely to take vitamins and more likely to rely on fast foods and fried foods. Healthy habits lead to other healthy choices — and soon, a healthy lifestyle is developed.

The Surgeon General has emphatically stated that being sedentary is a major risk factor for heart disease and other ills.

Inactivity is correlated with obesity, which is a growing problem for our country, and our children in particular, who, for the first time in our history, may have a shorter lifespan than their parents. We can't control certain risk factors such as family history, but we can control exercise, smoking, drinking, seatbelt wearing, vitamin usage, attitude, anger, and other variables that affect the quality of our lives.

Many people are digging their graves with their spoons and forks. Seven of the top ten killer diseases are associated with what we eat and how much of it. In particular, coronary artery disease, certain cancers, and diabetes can be created by our food choices. The key word there is "choices." Let me emphasize again that you are your choices. If you continue to make unhealthy choices, they will catch up to you both physiologically and psychologically. It's just a matter of time. You can only get away with it for so long. Most people finally get interested in healthy choices after the fact, e.g., after the heart attack or the diagnosis of cancer. Don't wait until then. There's no time like the present. In fact, give yourself a present by remembering to eat your vegetables, take your vitamins, wear your seatbelt, exercise, let go of anger, help others, and be kind to animals. And forget about smoking and eating or drinking to excess. Yes, give yourself that present, just for the health of it!

ME, ME, ME

In Greek mythology, there was a beautiful mountain nymph named Echo. She fell deeply in love with a very handsome young man by the name of Narcissus. Echo did all that she could to show her love for him, but not only was he uninterested, he cruelly rejected her by shouting, "I will die before you ever lie with me!"

Echo indulged her disappointment and sadness to the point where she resigned herself to being dispirited. Her rejection of life angered the gods, who condemned her to incessant wandering in the mountains where she could only repeat the last words of sentences that others spoke. However, she wanted revenge and asked the gods to punish Narcissus. Aphrodite decided to also make him the recipient of unrequited love.

So it was that Narcissus knelt over a lake to get water and saw his reflection. He fell in love. He tried in vain to embrace and kiss the handsome young man staring at him. Then, he realized it was himself. Enraptured, he stared at himself for many hours. He felt pain and sadness. The predicament was that he was seemingly incapable of loving another and that his love for himself was not interpersonal. Rollo May, writing in *Freedom and Destiny*, puts it this way:

> In grasping for freedom from entanglement with other persons, we come to grief over our failure of compassion and commitment—indeed, the failure to love authentically.

Narcissus continued to stare at his reflection and grew more and more preoccupied with his own beauty. He was so full of himself, there was no room for anyone else. He had no equal. If he could not possess himself, he felt destined to frustration and despair. That's when he killed himself, right at the spot where he was so consumed with himself. With his dying breath, he said, "Farewell, farewell." And Echo was able to say farewell. The beautiful flower Narcissus is named after him.

It is wonderful to have a good self image and have self-esteem. It's important to value yourself. It's fine to love yourself. But to be like Narcissus is tragic. To be overly consumed with yourself is a pretty good definition of neurosis. That preoccupation with yourself will interfere with your happiness and with your relationships. Recently, a professor who was dying gave her last lecture at the university. Her topic was "Get over yourself!"

MANAGING YOUR LIFE

How you manage your time (life) greatly determines how happy or unhappy you are. Stephen R. Covey offers the following time management matrix in his book *The 7 Habits of Highly Effective People*. I have taken the liberty of modifying it slightly.

	Urgent	Not Urgent
Important	**I** Crises Pressing problems Deadline-driven projects	**II** Meaningful projects Stress reduction Relationship building Recognizing new opportunities Planning Exercise Eating well
Not Important	**III** Other people's priorities Interruptions, some calls Some mail, some reports Some meetings Pressing matters Popular activities	**IV** Channel surfing Web surfing Trivia, busy work Some mail, some phone calls Time wasters Pleasant activities

Covey explains that the two variables defining any activity are "urgent" and "important." Urgent simply means that it's happening now and requires immediate attention. Something can be urgent but not important. Some urgent matters can even be fun and popular but still be unimportant (Quadrant III).

Importance has to do with anything that is directly related to your values, your high priority goals, and living a meaningful life. It's possible that things can be very important but have no sense of urgency (Quadrant II).

So, Quadrant I activities are urgent and important. Quadrant II activities are important but not urgent. Quadrant III activities are urgent but not important. And, Quadrant IV activities are neither urgent nor important.

Are you a Quadrant I person who seemingly is in crisis mode most of the time? How about a Quadrant III person who mistakenly believes all of her activities are urgent and important when they're most likely urgent and not important? Many people escape to Quadrant IV for mindless pleasure.

Here's the thing: if you're not feeling as good as you'd like and you're basically less than happy and feeling unfulfilled, you need to spend more and more time dealing with Quadrant II—that's the spot that can change your life. But the problem is that because there is no urgency there, you might not make the effort to do that. Psychotherapy is sometimes about taking what's in Quadrant II and moving it to Quadrant I. A person needs to learn how to say "yes" to the meaningful passions, projects, values, relationships, opportunities, and priorities of Quadrant II. This can be achieved by learning how to say "no" to many of the Quadrant III and Quadrant IV activities.

Whatever is in Quadrant II, try treating it as if it's urgent. Quadrant II is the guts of happiness. Quadrant IV is more akin to the appendix. By being more selective in III and IV and by sensing a note of urgency with respect to II, you can significantly change your life for the better and be a happier person.

> The key is not to prioritize
> what's on your schedule,
> but to schedule your priorities.
> –Stephen R. Covey

JUST A DREAM

Do you have any recurring dreams? Not necessarily the exact dream again and again, but perhaps a theme that shows up in many of your dreams? Recurring dreams are usually significant and contain valuable information about our lives. Pay attention to them. Many dreams are simply residue dreams, having more to do with the events of the last day or two. They are less important than any recurring dreams you may have.

For the past 30 years or more, I've had a recurring dream. It always feels great when I have it. I've had it recently. It begins with me walking, usually on city streets. Slowly, but surely, my steps get a little longer and I begin to spend a bit of time slightly off the ground with each step. My steps continue to get longer until I can go from the curb on one side of the street to the curb on the other side. It is the start of my getting higher and higher off the ground and into the air. I begin flying. No plane. Just me. No flapping of my arms. I'm hundreds of feet up in the air, feeling good and traveling light. It's a great feeling.

I'm guessing that I have these flying dreams about 10 times a year. They change slightly in content, but I'm always flying high and feeling exhilarated. Boundless. Free. In my last dream, flying high and surveying the landscape below, I saw one person alone in a grassy field. I felt drawn to get a closer look. As I descended, she looked up at me and smiled. It was my mother (who had died almost a decade ago). I smiled back. As I flew gently over her head, she reached up, and without a word, our hands met as we high-fived each other. It was a beautiful moment. I continued flying and that was the end of the dream.

What I like about the dream is the feeling that "the sky's the limit!" Tapping into my freedom, power, and faith, I allow myself to soar and delight in the adventure. The dream is not about being like Superman, but is about traveling light and trusting myself. It's about taking action and having a sense of wonder as well as accomplishment.

Are you stuck seeing things over and over from the same vantage point? How about giving yourself permission to fly and gaining a different perspective on your problems and your life? How about taking a chance on yourself?

> A bit of advice given to a young Native American at the time of his initiation: "As you go the way of life, you will see a great chasm. Jump. It is not as wide as you think."
>
> –Joseph Campbell

HOW MANY THERAPISTS DOES IT TAKE TO CHANGE A LIGHT BULB?

You have a light within you. Most of the time, it is dimly lit. Picture a lamp with a three-way bulb and how that operates. You can use the switch to go from low light to moderate or even brighter illumination. You control the switch. I'd say you have, at the least, a five-way light within you that ranges from being almost imperceptible to being a beautiful, high intensity, radiant beacon. I want you to be able to access your light, because there's tremendous power and energy there.

Let there be light.
–God

May the longtime
Sun shine 'pon you,
all love surround you

and the pure light within you
guide your way home.
–The Incredible String Band

Despite having this wonderful resource within us, we still tend to lose our way in the dark. It is natural to fumble around and to stumble—that is indeed part of the dance. But, if we remember to turn on our light, the path we need to take becomes clearer and easier to negotiate. We all have to find our own way out of the dark forest.

Your inner light is not just there for the difficult times. It's always there ready to be utilized and maximized. If you remember that it's there and decide to actualize it and bring it to your day-to-day happenings and relationships, it will bring you brighter days and make you happier. For some reason, we seem more likely to stay in the dark, so to speak. Marianne Williamson says:

> It is our light, not our darkness, that frightens us. We ask ourselves, "Who am I to be brilliant, gorgeous, talented, fabulous?" Actually, who are you not to be?

I would add:

> "Who am I to be happy, satisfied, curious, passionate, grateful, involved, optimistic?" Actually, who are you not to be?

The greatest danger for most of us is not
that our aim is too high and we miss it,
but that it is too low and we reach it.
–Michaelangelo

III.
THINKING
&
ATTENTION

If you cannot get rid of the family skeleton,
you may as well make it dance.
–George Bernard Shaw

THE COMPARISON TRAP

I work with some people who spend a lot of time comparing themselves to others—unfavorably. These people are relentless at finding fault with themselves and thinking others are better than them. Typically, they are lousy evaluators of both themselves and others. By elevating others, they diminish themselves.

> If your compassion does
> not include yourself,
> it is incomplete.
> –Buddha

Steve is a World War II veteran and served honorably but believes he's inferior because he wasn't a fighter pilot and didn't see a lot of action. He worked steadily for 35 years for a major chain store and achieved manager of his department. He feels inadequate because he never got to be manager of the whole store. Steve feels like he's not good enough and believes others are better than him. He compares himself to others constantly, although there is really no reason to do this.

It is not necessary for
crows to be eagles.
–Sitting Bull

I frequently remind Steve that no one in his life is telling him he's not good enough — not a boss or a spouse or anyone. His totally self-inflicted trip is taking him in the wrong direction. He fears being unsuccessful, so he doesn't try many things. Sometimes, he feels immobilized or overwhelmed. I remind him that it's not as important for him to be the fighter pilot as it is for him to be the best Steve that he's capable of being.

Once the game is over,
the King and the pawn
go back in the same box.
–Italian Proverb

I think, above all, Steve wants to matter, to make a difference. I applaud that. I think we all want to matter. But Steve is wasting time worrying about his perceived inadequacies. He is discouraging himself. There's no time for that. We have no time to lose. Every moment counts. I have Steve hug himself daily and say "I love you" to himself. Steve needs to stop comparing himself with others and start valuing himself. Life is not easy. Give yourself a break!

Newborns aren't lying around the hospital nursery checking out who's thinner or who has the most hair. And toddlers who play together aren't trying to figure out whose blocks are imported from Germany and whose are hand-me-downs.

–Stephen M. Pollan and Mark Levine

ACCENTUATE THE POSITIVE

Decades ago, the great songwriters Johnny Mercer and Harold Arlen penned a hit tune that became a pop standard:

> You've got to accentuate the positive
> Eliminate the negative
> Latch on to the affirmative
> Don't mess with Mister In-Between
>
> You've got to spread joy up to the maximum
> Bring gloom down to the minimum
> Have faith or pandemonium
> Liable to walk upon the scene

About 10 years ago, Dr. Martin Seligman had a related epiphany having to do with the field of psychology:

> The most important thing, the most gen-
> eral thing I learned, was that psychology
> was half-baked, literally half-baked. We
> had baked the part about mental illness;
> we had baked the part about repair of
> damage .... The other side's unbaked, the
> side of strength, the side of what we're
> good at.

In other words, psychology emphasized pathology. It focused
on what's wrong with people and how to get them to feel somewhat better. As Seligman puts it, it's like getting them to go
from a minus-five to a minus-three. He was more interested in
a psychology that would take you to a plus-seven or higher. He
recognized the importance of studying "the strengths and virtues
that enable individuals and communities to thrive." Instead of
concentrating on mental illness, he proposed we research and
promote mental wellness. This was the birth of what has become
known as Positive Psychology.

This theory posits that there are three overlapping tiers
that contribute to happiness. Tier one is about pleasure, fun,
and enjoyment. For example, eating an ice cream cone, seeing
a good movie, or having sex are tier one players in the happiness formula. The second tier has to do with the depth of true
engagement that you bring to your pursuits and relationships.
For example, having good friends, loving someone deeply, and
wholeheartedly pursuing a course of study or career are tier
two ingredients in the formula. Tier three has to do with living
a meaningful life or a "life of affiliation." Here, a person finds
meaning and purpose by believing in and connecting to and giving back to something larger and more permanent than herself.

For example, nature, a religion, an ethnic group, an organization or movement that she believes in, God, spirituality, and so on.

Tier three is where it comes together. Pleasure is fine, but in and of itself, it's what Seligman calls the fidgeting-to-death syndrome. Being engaged in life is crucial, but probably not enough to bring about true satisfaction, contentment, and joy. Ideally, you can incorporate all three tiers in a balanced way to achieve optimal functioning and happiness.

I'm sure it's obvious why happiness is so important. Many studies have definitively demonstrated that positive emotions are significantly related to health, well-being, disability-free living, and a lengthier life span. It feels good to be a positive person. You will like yourself better and other people will also like you better. Of course, there are exceptions to every rule and theorem, but positive emotions are likely to increase both the quality and quantity of your life.

> Consult not your fears, but your hopes and dreams. Think not about your frustrations, but about your unfulfilled potential. Concern yourself not with what you tried and failed in, but with what is still possible for you to do.
>
> –Pope John XXIII

See Positive Psych 101 in Appendix A on page 263.

WOULD YOU LIKE
THAT SUPER-SIZED?

Buddhism reveals how life's usual pains, losses, predicaments, and dilemmas are worsened by our minds. We're experts at turning pain into suffering. We're filled with regret or guilt about the past, irrationally pursue pleasure in the present, and worry about the future. We become proficient at making things more emotionally difficult than they need to be.

Robert Sapolsky of Stanford University calls this "adventitious suffering." This means that humans, unlike other mammals, layer optional distress atop inevitable pain. We think about things in such a way so as to make the situation worse than it needs to be. We deal with the pain of what was, what is, and what could be, sometimes simultaneously. It is painful enough to lose a job or a lover, but we tend to add to our pains and burdens with our mind's rantings and ruminations. Adventitious means extra. If you ordered at McDonald's, they would ask, "Would you like that super-sized?" If you say yes, you get a lot more than if you say no. Emotional pain is similar. Our natural tendency is to feel the pain and automatically tell our mind to "super-size it."

For example, the pain of losing a job is exacerbated when you dwell on:

> –Regretting taking the job
> –Wasting the last four years
> –Being unemployed
> –Being seen as a failure
> –Worrying about getting a job
> –Worrying about finding a job you like
> –Worrying about your future pay
> –Fearing future failure
> –Thinking of other disappointments in your life
> –Whether you'll be able to pay your bills
> –Not being able to buy that new car
> –Not getting treated fairly
> –Getting revenge on your old boss

You can see how the pain of losing the job can turn into adventitious suffering. It's been said that pain is inevitable, but suffering is optional. Suffering occurs when we take the pain and super-size it. When you're about to do that, catch yourself in the act and say, "No, thank you." Recognize when enough is enough.

(Our minds make the wolf bigger than he is.)

PULL THE PLUG

We can be bluffed by our own thoughts. This happens when we take our thoughts too literally or too seriously. They're just thoughts. Let me repeat that, because it's important for you to understand. They're just thoughts. That's it. They have no particular power or influence over you, that is, unless you decide to invest in them, indulge them, believe them, and allow them to frighten you. This indulgence leads to anxiety or depression.

When I see people in therapy who believe and emotionally invest in unproductive thoughts, I tell them something akin to the following: "I'm doing therapy with you in this office. You're telling me about issues in your life. Suppose I suddenly get the thought that I'm going to stand up and jump out of my office window. Now, I can relate to this in a couple of different ways. The first possibility is that I can tell myself that I'm losing my mind or losing control. I can believe that and begin to feel disoriented and on the brink of irrational and impulsive behavior.

I begin to feel anxiety and agitation. And, I certainly have lost contact with you as I've not been hearing what you've been saying. So, I'm doing both a poor job of dealing with my thoughts and being your therapist."

I continue by telling the person, "But suppose I get that same thought about standing up and jumping out of my office window and I relate to it very differently. Now I simply tell myself that it's just a thought and I don't have to believe it. In essence, I pull the plug on it, so there's no emotional charge connected to the thought. It has no power to influence. It's just a thought and I'm not bluffed by it. Therefore, I don't actually fear getting up and jumping out the window. I let the thought go and continue to focus on you and what you're saying. In this way, I do a good job of both dealing with my thoughts and being your therapist."

So keep in mind that you don't have to believe everything you think and you certainly don't have to indulge anxiety-provoking or depressing thoughts. Pull the plug and be an energy saver. This way, you'll be able to use that saved energy for more productive thoughts and pursuits.

OCCAM'S RAZOR

I'd like you to try your hand at writing some haiku poetry. Here's why: I'm a great advocate for not complicating your life. I want you to learn to be a simplifier rather than a complicator. We are ingenious. We find all sorts of ways to make things more difficult than they need to be. We're experts at making the proverbial straight arrow crooked. Writing haiku is a way of practicing not adding anything extra or unnecessary. It is a simple form of poetry that requires disciplined thinking and non-embellishment.

The traditional haiku consists of three lines, all referring to one moment in time—the present moment. When you begin composing, it may be helpful to stick to the widely accepted form of five syllables in the first line, seven syllables in the second, and five in the third. So, when haiku is taught, it is almost always presented in that 5-7-5 format. If you don't count syllables, just write about one moment in time using three lines. Do not use rhyme, embellishment, metaphor, simile, or any other poetic devices you may have learned. Keep it simple. Here are some examples:

> bordertown:
> breastfeeding mother
> asks for a handout

> now and again
> out of a hole in the ice
> a seal's head

> drought:
> creakdust
> stillness

> junkyard:
> crows in
> a '53 Chevy

> snowed in:
> aduki beans soaking on
> a potbelly stove

> spring afternoon
> on each end of the park bench
> an old man sleeps

> spring rain ...
> reading Ecclesiastes
> in the motel bed

In the 14th century, an English Franciscan friar, William of Ockham, cemented his legacy as one of the major figures of medieval times by introducing a principle of logic that sparked debate in the worlds of science and theology. This principle has come to be known as Occam's Razor. It has to do with parsimony and not unnecessarily inventing theories or entities to explain something. In essence, Occam's Razor is used to shave off any constructs, thoughts, theories, and whatever else that isn't really needed to explain the phenomenon you're dealing with. As Freud was once reported to utter, "Sometimes a cigar is just a cigar."

Our minds are characteristically anti-parsimonious. In fact, they typically create complex and complicated thoughts and explanations that interfere with our well-being. As I said, we are complicators. Meditation or writing haiku helps us to learn how to use Occam's Razor in such a way so we are creating less anxiety and depression. Catch yourself when you're making too many assumptions, doing too much embellishing, and overthinking. Remind yourself to think haiku-like and use Occam's Razor to shave away unnecessary obstructions to your well-being.

AAA

When most people hear the term "Triple A" or see AAA, they think of the Automobile Association of America. Its function is to provide "trip tickets" or routes travelers can take, and also provide rescue services for those in need of towing or car repair. AAA has helped countless people get to where they wanted to go.

I have my own version of AAA that I use when working as a therapist. In this case, the *As* don't stand for Automobile Association of America, but the goal is the same — to help people find their way and get where they want to go. My AAA stands for:

–Attention
–Amplitude
–Attitude

This AAA is also a vehicle that can rescue you from anxiety, depression, and other places of stuckness. Just like a disabled car, you may be stuck and unable to get out of the rut that prevents you from feeling better. Triple A to the rescue.

Attention

How you feel and whether you are happy or unhappy, anxiety-ridden or relatively relaxed, depends on what you pay attention to. I've often said to my patients, "If I spent all day focusing on the same things you do, I'd be miserable too!" What is your mind attending to? A guy I know spends much of his time watching cable news channels that parade an endless stream of ills and tragedies all day and night. I'm not surprised he chronically struggles with a low-grade depression. A woman continually attends to her perceived unfair treatment at the hands of her children and other family members. She also pays a lot of attention to what others have that she doesn't, grappling with feelings of inadequacy and inferiority.

Amplitude

If you were listening to a song on the radio that was annoying and aggravating, would you turn up the volume? Unless you're masochistic, I'm assuming you answered no. You would either turn the volume way down or, more likely, switch to a different station. If you find that you're attending to negative thoughts, catch yourself in the act. Don't continue to indulge the negativity by getting more involved with it. Recognize it for what it is and turn it down. Better yet, after you've tuned in to the fact of attending to it, turn it off. Make the conscious effort to switch stations.

Attitude

Having a poor attitude equates to having a disability. Your attitude will make your world bleak or Technicolor. Optimism or pessimism? "I'll give it a try" or "I'll never be able to do it"? Hopefulness versus hopelessness. It's been said that attitude determines altitude. Are you excited about life and the wondrous possibilities, or are you bored? Are you frightened of the world because it is a dangerous place, or are you ready to explore? Do you choose an attitude leading to miserable safety or one of willingness to risk? Do you count your problems or your blessings?

If you're emotionally stuck in a place of negativity—be it fear, unhappiness, insecurity, low self-esteem, anger, and so on—you're in need of rescue. Call AAA—and I don't mean the Automobile Association of America.

JUST SHUT UP

Sometimes we can overthink things. This usually is unproductive. The noted writer and poet Natalie Goldberg has written about her own overthinking when she first got on the spiritual path. She was obsessing about trees and asked her teacher if elm trees suffer. He gave her a straight answer. That was not good enough. She continued:

> "What? Could you please tell me again?
> Do they really suffer?" I couldn't take it in.
>
> He shot back his reply.
>
> It pinged off my forehead and did not penetrate. I was caught in my thinking mind, too busy trying to understand everything. But my confusion had drive. I raised my hand a third time.

"Roshi, just once more. I don't get it. I mean do trees really suffer?"

He looked straight at me. "Shut up."

That went in.

She went on to say that the question about the elm trees stopped grabbing her by the throat. The term "monkey mind" refers to when the mind is racing and producing a preponderance of thoughts involving a myriad of subjects. In essence, monkey mind is on one end of the continuum with peace of mind being on the other. Overthinking and lack of focus produce monkey mind.

My hunch is that overthinking and happiness have an inverse relationship. The more you overthink, the less happy you'll probably be. So, quiet down. Catch yourself in the act when you're ruminating, obsessing, or producing too many thoughts or mind noise. Then, in your mind's eye, visualize one or more of the following three signs:

No Monkey Mind

No Disturbing the Peace

and finally

Just Shut Up!

IV.
FREEDOM
&
RESPONSIBILITY

Instead of seeing the rug being pulled from under us,
we can learn to dance on the shifting carpet.
–Thomas Crum

IN AND OUT OF THE TRAP

Patients frequently tell me that they feel trapped. Can you relate to that? Trapped in a relationship, or maybe in a job? Like there's no way out? Like Sartre's "No Exit"? Listen carefully. The trap is an illusion. Maybe you think that I don't understand, that you really are trapped. Well, as compassionate as I am to your plight, I still respectfully beg to differ. I will not say that you are trapped. What I will say is that you have very difficult choices. With so many possible mitigating or extenuating circumstances attached to your situation, it may indeed feel as if you have no options. But you do. That is important for you to know and believe. If you don't, you'll feel powerless and hopeless.

Some choices are excruciatingly hard to make. It may be easier to feel trapped and do nothing than to choose to get out of the trap and deal with the consequences as well as with the unknown. Known misery may be preferable. In making difficult choices, you will probably have to confront intense ambivalence, grapple with guilt, and risk the disapproval of important people in your life. As horrible as it feels to be trapped, you might be choosing that rather than having to face the burden and consequences of exercising your freedom.

We can have this argument for a long time. You'll insist that you're trapped and will offer me a myriad of proofs to that effect. I'll insist that you have choices that will get you out of the trap, albeit with the caveats of facing the anxiety-provoking unknown as well as the loss of the known. I'll remind you how resilient you are and that you're capable of doing extremely difficult things. But the bottom line is that it's your choice. I just want you to understand and believe that you have a choice. What you ultimately decide to choose is up to you, and you only. However, if you choose to stay in the trap, is it really a trap?

> The image that often comes to mind is from cowboy movies of the 1940s, where a sheriff puts a rowdy person in a jail cell and shuts the door but doesn't lock it. The joke is that the prisoner shouts and rattles the bars of the cell while the audience knows he needs only to turn the handle in order to get out.
> –Sylvia Boorstein

TURN AROUND

You can drive yourself crazy. It's really not that hard to do. I've seen countless people do it. You can drive yourself to depression. May I make a suggestion? Turn around. You're driving in the wrong direction! You need a new map.

It takes even more energy to drive yourself crazy than it does to drive yourself sane. It takes more energy to drive yourself to depression than to drive yourself to happiness. If you want to feel better, first you have to realize that you've been driving in the wrong direction. Accept responsibility for where you are. Make the decision to turn around. Now.

It's been said that what is most important is not the hand you're dealt but how you play it. Jim was telling me a story about his father who remained happy and smiling, even after 20 years as a caretaker for Jim's mother who had a debilitating muscular disease. During those years, the father had to put his career as a jazz musician on hold.

Jim:	Dad, why the hell are you always happy?
Father:	I choose to be. It sure beats the alternative.

Jim's father could have easily driven himself crazy. Instead, he decided to drive himself sane. We're always driving ourselves somewhere. You need to accept responsibility for the direction you're heading in and how you are feeling. Don't blame others. Don't tell me that you're incapable of change. Take responsibility.

A 79-year-old grandmother from New Mexico ordered a cup of coffee from the McDonald's drive-through. With the car parked, she put the coffee cup between her knees to open it so as to add cream and sugar. Doing so, the whole cup of coffee spilled on her lap. She sat in the puddle of coffee for over 90 seconds and suffered burns that required hospitalization and skin grafting. She sued McDonald's. The jury awarded her millions of dollars. On appeal, the parties settled out of court for an amount thought to be in the neighborhood of $600,000. Am I missing something?

Do you remember the "Twinkie defense"? In 1979, a man assassinated two men, including the mayor of San Francisco. As part of his defense, the lawyers and psychiatrists cited that he had been struggling with depression and had been regularly consuming Twinkies and Coca-Cola. Now, I understand that might not be the breakfast of champions, but were the Twinkies really responsible for the killings? The defense lawyers were able to have the killer's charges reduced from murder to manslaughter based on diminished capacity (with the assumption that the Twinkies contributed to the diminished capacity to plan a premeditated murder).

So, I'm asking you to take responsibility for the direction

you're going in. If you're headed in the wrong direction, stop. Design a new map. Please don't sue McDonald's or invoke the Twinkie defense.

THE MAGIC BULLET

You might be taken aback by the number of people who, early on in therapy, ask me for "the magic bullet." Others say, "Can't you just press the magic button?" Then there are those who ask me to hypnotize them, find out what's wrong, fix it, and not even tell them what it was. I'll usually break the news to them gently by saying something to the effect of, "There is no magic bullet. I'll help you get through this. I'll do my part, but you have to stop seeking magic and start taking responsibility for how you feel. In all likelihood, you are the problem, and you are the solution."

Many people are not thrilled by this revelation. They would prefer the magic. Robin was always asking me to fix her. She came in one day feeling more distressed than usual. She related a dream in which she signed herself out of the "insane asylum." The insane asylum frightened her as she related it to being "crazy." I helped her to see this as a positive and empowering dream. Instead of waiting for someone to rescue her or continuing to see herself as a victim, she took action and signed herself out. This was the beginning of Robin's accepting responsibility. Our task was to clarify what the insane asylum represented. Was it work, a relationship, a lifestyle, a personality trait, or her attitude? Did the asylum symbolize her fear connected to there not being a magic bullet and her remaining ill?

There is the old story about the student who approaches the Zen master and says, "Master, please set me free!"

The wise Zen sage replies, "But who has you in bondage?"

If you wait for the magic bullet, the miracle, the guru, or the like, you may have a very long wait. Take a hint from Robin. Start taking responsibility. Sign yourself out of the insane asylum.

EAT YOUR LUNCH

In *It's Easier Than You Think*, Sylvia Boorstein provides the following account of a plane trip she took:

> Many, many years ago, when I was in my early twenties and flying in an airplane was still a novelty to me, I flew to New York City from Atlanta, Georgia. It was a rainy day, and the propeller plane didn't fly above the weather so we bounced around a lot. I gripped the arms of my seat, clenched my teeth, took my pulse a lot, and counted the minutes until landing. The "older woman" in the seat next to me (a woman probably my current age) sat impassively, accepted the flight attendant's offer of lunch, and ate it. "How

come she isn't frightened?" I thought
to myself. When we touched down on
the runway in New York, I whispered,
"Thank God!" She turned to me and
smiled. "You said it!" she replied. What
a piece of news that was to me. She had
been frightened, too, but she had eaten
her lunch.

In my twenties, I had a drug-induced psychotic episode
shortly before flying to Maine to be interviewed for a staff psychologist position at a hospital. The psychiatrist who interviewed
me for hours had a long, dark beard. I was delusional and hal-
lucinatory throughout the interview as he morphed back and
forth from man to wolfman. Half of the time, he spoke. The other
half, he growled and roared. I was terrified. When the interview
ended, he offered me the job. Later in this book, you'll read a
story about it.

When we are frightened, we still need to find a way to deal
with what's going on. What's the alternative? Falling apart
doesn't really solve much of anything. No need to scold yourself
if you are scared or devastated. That's okay. Just remember to
do what you need to do, and eat your lunch.

> Just because you are seeing divine light,
> experiencing waves of bliss, or conversing
> with Gods and Godesses is no reason not
> to know your zip code.
>
> –Ram Dass

Alan Gettis, Ph.D.

Courage is being scared to death—
but still saddling up.
–John Wayne

A NO-WIN SITUATION

In 279 BC, King Pyrrhus of Epirus defeated the Romans during the Pyrrhic War at Asculum. It was the second casualty-filled battle with the Romans in a short period of time. His best soldiers and chief commanders were killed, as were many of his troops. Afterward, Pyrrhus said, "Another such victory over the Romans and we are undone." The term "Pyrrhic victory" has come to be known as a victory that has a devastating cost to the victor.

We are not only referring to military battles. A Pyrrhic victory also applies to politics, sports, business, and many other arenas. As a therapist, I have frequently heard about and have sometimes witnessed this phenomenon in relationships. For example, a husband might attain a Pyrrhic victory over his wife. This is a very sad thing. It is traumatic for both of them. Things may never be the same for them again. When you know someone intimately, you know much about her, including her insecurities, history, and vulnerabilities. These can become targets as words are used like ammunition, piercing the heart and spirit of the defeated.

There is a high cost to the health of a relationship in any Pyrrhic victory. Trust is shattered. Foundations crumble. Anger and resentment breed with the hurt and wounds festering underneath. I frequently ask people, "Would you rather win or would you rather be happy?" Be careful with going for the jugular. It's generally a terrible idea. Err on the side of biting your tongue, buying time by going for a walk, and rethinking how to get your points across. A war of words will only lead to a Pyrrhic victory, and in that victory, everyone loses.

> Douglas Steere, a Quaker teacher, says that the ancient question, "Who am I?" inevitably leads to a deeper one, "Whose am I?" — because there is no identity outside of relationship. You can't be a person by yourself. To ask "Whose am I?" is to extend the question far beyond the little self-absorbed self, and wonder: Who needs you? Who loves you? To whom are you accountable? To whom do you answer? Whose life is altered by your choices? With whose life, whose lives, is your own all bound up, inextricably, in obvious or invisible ways?
>
> –The Rev. Victoria Safford

AHA

Rollo May defines freedom as "the capacity to pause in the midst of stimuli from all directions, and in this pause to throw our weight toward this response rather than that one." Think about that carefully. Freedom is found in the pause between stimulus and response. Wow. The power in that pause. It's the pause that breaks conditioned behaviors, conditioned thoughts, and conditioned feelings. It's no longer stimulus / response. Now it's stimulus / pause + decide consciously (rather than exist on automatic pilot) how you want to respond / response. Freedom of choice.

That pause is pregnant with possibilities. In the freedom of that pause, you can change your life. When the bestselling author Stephen R. Covey first encountered this idea, he was immediately transformed:

My office was on the outside edge of a college, and one day as I was wandering between stacks of books in the back of the college library, I came across a book that drew my interest. As I opened it, my eyes fell upon a single paragraph that powerfully influenced the rest of my life.

I read the paragraph over and over again. It basically contained the simple idea that there is a gap or a space between stimulus and response, and that the key to both our growth and happiness is how we use that space.

I can hardly describe the effect that idea had on my mind. Though I had been nurtured in the philosophy of self-determinism, the way the idea was phrased — "a gap between stimulus and response" — hit me with fresh, almost unbelievable force. It was almost like "knowing it for the first time," like an inward revolution, "an idea whose time had come."

He did not overreact. The idea has had a similar impact on my life. I think it is the most liberating and empowering idea in psychology. Read it again. And again. Digest it. We could just as easily say that happiness is found in the pause between stimulus and response. The freedom to be happier and change your life is contained in that pause. That's a lot of responsibility clearly placed upon your shoulders. Some people find it too burdensome. Like Kierkegaard said, "Anxiety is the dizziness of freedom." Therefore, some people would prefer not to get this idea. They'd prefer same old, same old. They'd opt for helplessness, dependency, victimization, denial, security (even if it's miserable), anger, anxiety, dysthymia, boredom, and existential despair.

What will it be for you? Read about the pause again. Do you get it? Is it liberating, fear-provoking, or both? You might want to pause before you answer.

ON FALLING FROM GRACE

In the 21st century, it is getting harder and harder to find role models. The bigger they are, the harder they fall. Tiger Woods, George W. Bush—one by one, they increasingly go by the wayside. Sports heroes, movie stars, politicians, presidents, and even religious and spiritual leaders have had their turn falling from grace. It is disheartening to find that these famous people who we have cheered for, looked up to, admired, and respected, continue to disappoint us. They beat their wives, lie, cheat, become addicted to drugs, commit sexual abuse, drive while under the influence, commit various other crimes, and are markedly egocentric.

There is a principle known as the "halo effect." Studies have show that if you show people pictures of very attractive women or men and ask them to rate those pictured along various dimensions, the attractive people will be judged to be nice, sincere, trustworthy, smart, and so on. These attributes are not ascribed to people pictured who are much less attractive.

I guess that's part of the reason we are still so surprised when one of the stars of our society, so to speak, is found out. We still think that, because he is handsome or rich and powerful, he is automatically an all-around wonderful person. Evidence the halo effect. Maybe we need to accept that these people are just fallible human beings like all of us, but perhaps with additional burdens that accompany fame and fortune. I think we'd have better luck looking for role models closer to home. What about the local brownie leader, the teacher who goes the extra mile, the guy who's worked that 9-to-5 job for the past 30 years, the neighbor who always offers to watch your place when you're away, the nitty-gritty day-to-day people who quietly take care of people, provide services in a responsible manner, take pride in whatever it is they do in the community, and treat others like they themselves would want to be treated.

Those people, generous of spirit and in action, are the real role models. My father offered me the following bit of wisdom: "Always do right and you'll never go wrong." Although it's easier said than done, now is the time to heed that advice. It really amounts to being able to look up to yourself. It doesn't matter if you've done things in the past that you feel ashamed of or embarrassed about. From this point on, don't do anything that will compromise your values or jeopardize you legally, psychologically, ethically, or spiritually. It's just not worth it.

In the Kabbalah, there is the myth of the Tikkun Olam, which believes that it is our responsibility to repair the world. We all have a spark of divine light deep within us waiting to be discovered and manifested. Through kindness, love, and compassion, we begin to relate to ourselves and others in such a way that we help restore the holiness of the world. We liberate our sparks of divinity and do our best to raise the sparks of others. This gathering of and igniting of the fragmented sparks helps to restore the wholeness and holiness of the world, while helping us to try our best not to fall from grace. By the way, the word "holy" is of French derivation from the same word root as health, happiness, and wholeness. Webster defines it as being spiritually whole or sound. Restoring holiness is a pretty good thing to do. What you do matters. Your attitude and actions can make a difference in the world.

THE GNAWING

There is a wonderful Cheyenne story that was told by Mrs. Medicine Bull in Birney, Montana, with the help of an interpreter. It was recorded by Richard Erdoes. I have adapted it slightly:

> There is a great pole somewhere, a mighty trunk similar to the sacred sundance pole, only much, much bigger. This pole is what holds up the world. The Great White Grandfather Beaver of the North is gnawing at that pole. He has been gnawing at the bottom of it for ages and ages. More than half of the pole has already been gnawed through. When the Great White Beaver of the North gets angry, he gnaws faster and more furiously. Once he has gnawed all the way through, the pole

will topple, and the earth will crash into a
bottomless nothing. That will be the end
of the people—of everything. The end of
all ends. So we are careful not to make the
Beaver angry. We want the world to last
a little longer.

I guess it's important to figure out what gets the Beaver angry. Try to figure out what you believe would upset the Great
White Grandfather Beaver of the North. I have my own ideas that
I'll share with you. Perusing animal symbolism and native art
suggests that the Beaver was considered an old, wise, and compassionate creature. He showed the people how to cut down trees
and build houses so they would be safe and warm in the winter.
Beavers are associated with hard work. They're industrious and
persevere with incredible will and patience. They are deemed to
be noble and honest and creative. They are monogamous.

With that in mind, here's a partial list of what I think might
greatly annoy the Beaver:

> –Impatience
> –Sloth, laziness, and lack of effort
> –Doing harm to the environment
> –Being harmful to others rather than helpful
> –Not taking on difficult challenges
> –Dishonesty
> –Infidelity
> –Being unimaginative or uninspired
> –Boredom
> –Being mean-spirited
> –Engaging in destructive or self-destructive behavior

I would like the world to last a little longer. If I don't anger the Beaver, I'll be doing my part and chances are I'll feel pretty good in the process. Can I count on you to help me and the rest of the world? Please, do not anger the Beaver!

You can dance anywhere,
even if only in your heart.

V.
GRATITUDE
&
KINDNESS

In life as in dance,
grace glides on blistered feet.
–Alice Abrams

CENTER STAGE

Don always seemed to need to draw attention to himself. It was as if anything you could do, he could do better. You could never tell a story without Don following it with a bigger and better version. If you saw a rainbow, he saw a double rainbow. If you had lunch with your boss, he had dinner with the CEO. He was a chronic name dropper and would frequently only use the first names of stars, such as Leo (Leonardo DiCaprio) or Julia (Roberts). I once remarked to him that, surprisingly enough, the best Chinese food I ever had was in Mexico. He immediately countered that the best Chinese food he ever had was in China. You get the picture.

Now, I understand that we all have needs that need to be satisfied, and that the need to be attended to is a basic, universal one. But everyone should have a turn. While others are sharing their feelings and experiences, you have the choice of drawing them out or shifting the emphasis to yourself. Practice not only letting someone else have center stage, but actually helping them to do so. It doesn't diminish you if someone else is in the spotlight. You'll get your turn in due time. It's not necessary to fight for air time. Just gracefully allow the other person some time and space to express himself.

I'd like you to do an experiment. Forget about yourself for a day. Devote one day to helping everyone you come in contact with feel a little bit better. Through your words and your actions, give people a contact high. Almost all of us have experienced a person somewhere who affects people that way. Someone who is cheerful, looks you in the eye, and treats you like she's genuinely interested in you rather than robotically uttering the catch phrase of "Have a nice day."

Start by saying "Good morning!" and "How are you?" with feeling and with interest. Ask questions of the people you have your daily interactions with. Be interested in them. Really listen to what they have to say. Find something to compliment them about. Inquire as to their health or how their family members are doing. Take a day off from voicing your own concerns or focusing upon yourself. Let others be the center of attention. Nurture them. Create an interchange or an atmosphere that they can bask in and feel uplifted.

In helping them feel good, you may even feel a bit better yourself. After you are the antithesis of Narcissus for a day, reflect upon the experience. You were uplifting to other people and did nothing to diminish yourself. You gave freely and it didn't cost you a thing. John Andrew Holmes has said that there is no exercise better for the heart than reaching down and lifting people up.

WATER, WATER, EVERYWHERE

In his landmark book, *The Hidden Messages in Water*, Dr. Masaru Emoto, the renowned Japanese scientist, uses high-speed photography to show that water molecules are greatly affected by words, thoughts, and feelings. Let me explain the important ramifications of this study as it relates to humans, who as it turns out, exist mostly as water.

The fetus is roughly 99 percent water. The newborn is about 90 percent. The adult human is approximately 70 percent water. If you are fortunate to die of old age, you'll be made up of around 50 percent water. Dr. Emoto discovered that frozen spring water that was exposed to loving words produced crystals of intricate, attractive, and colorful snowflake patterns. Just the opposite was true of polluted water and water exposed to negative thoughts, which produced crystals of dull colors and fragmented, distorted shapes.

Here's a specific example: When water was exposed to the

words "love" and "gratitude," the frozen crystals resulted in photographs that evidenced symmetry and beauty. When water was exposed to negative words such as "stupid" and "Satan," the photographs of the frozen crystals showed broken shapes and flawed formations. The actual pictures are startling. Water exposed to Mozart's "40th Symphony in G Minor" (one of my favorites) resulted in delicate and elegant crystals, while the water exposed to violent heavy metal music resulted in mal-formed crystals.

The important idea is this: if words and thoughts can change the basic structure of water, and we are comprised mostly of water, our words and thoughts about ourselves and the words others expose us to can have a profound impact upon our health and well-being or the lack of it. Some people have taken to label-ing their bottled water with tags having words on them such as "beauty," "kindness," "love," and "gratitude."

Dr. Emoto summarizes his findings as follows:

How will you choose to live your life?

If you fill your heart with love and grati-tude, you will find yourself surrounded by so much that you can love and that you can feel grateful for, and you can even get closer to enjoying the life of health and happiness that you seek. But what will happen if you emit signals of hate, dis-satisfaction, and sadness? Then you will probably find yourself in a situation that makes you hateful, dissatisfied, and sad. The life you live and the world you live in are up to you.

1944

I don't remember the following experience. After all, I was only a few months old. But I'll tell it to you as I've heard it from my parents and siblings. I was hospitalized with a condition that the doctors were unable to diagnose. My body had become hard with areas from head to foot that looked and felt like rocks. In the hospital, the staff referred to me as "stone boy." I had a bluish cast. Story has it that I was unresponsive to treatment. The doctor told my parents that it was likely I would die. My sister was wracked with guilt. The day before I took ill, she wanted to wake me so that she could play with me. She pinched me hard while I was asleep in my crib. She thought the pinch caused me to turn to stone.

As I grew closer to death, one of the physicians told my parents he was going to try a brand new drug that the army had started using with the soldiers fighting in World War II to deal with their infections stemming from their battle wounds. They gave me the drug. It saved my life. That new drug was penicillin.

Fast forward to 2010. I'm making a house call to see Don, an 85-year-old gentleman who I always look forward to seeing. We began to talk of his army days and his war experiences. He was 19 and was an infantry soldier. Continually on the move, he went from Africa to Italy, and that's where it happened: wounded in action. They had to do a guillotine amputation and this teenage boy was transferred to a stateside hospital. It turns out that the "hospital" was actually a hotel in Atlantic City that was transposed into a military hospital. Don spent a year there with a couple of thousand other amputees, learning how to adjust to life with one leg. He told me that his original wounds led to complications, and that it was a new drug, penicillin, that had saved his life. That's when I shared my stone boy experience with him.

So, here it was that 66 years later, two men whose lives were saved because of a new drug were able to have the lives they've had and share these moments with each other, here and now. Stone boy and the amputee agreed — they felt gratitude for penicillin and for the lives they have had since 1944.

JOHNNY B. GOODE

The noted psychologist Daniel Goleman makes a convincing case that we humans are innately disposed to kindness and empathy. He believes that we are hardwired for altruism. In fact, scientists have traced the beginnings of morality to other primates. Biologists and primatologists have advanced the viewpoint that morality preceded religion by thousands of years. Acting morally was adaptive and increased chances of survival. Religion came later to provide context, rituals, and a narrative that houses moral behavior.

Goleman cites the following as being illustrations of instinctive compassion:

> Six rhesus monkeys have been trained
> to pull chains to get food. At one point
> a seventh monkey, in full view of the
> others, gets a painful shock whenever

one of them pulls for food. On seeing the pain of that shocked monkey, four of the original rhesus monkeys start pulling a different chain, one that delivers less food to them but that inflicts no shock on the other monkey. The fifth monkey stops pulling any chain at all for five days, and the sixth for twelve days—that is, both starve themselves to prevent shocking the seventh monkey.

and

Virtually from birth, when babies see or hear another baby crying in distress, they start crying as though they too are distressed. But they rarely cry when they hear a recording of their own cries. After about fourteen months of age, babies not only cry when they hear another, but they also try to relieve the other baby's suffering somehow. The older toddlers get, the less they cry and the more they try to help.

This hardwiring for altruism is reinforced when we see or hear about acts of courage and kindness. Witnessing someone else's compassionate or helping actions brings about a feeling that psychologists term "elevation." It's a good feeling that leads to wanting to do something kind or compassionate. It's contagious.

If it's built into our neural architecture to be this way, why aren't we like this all the time? It seems that certain things can short circuit our hardwiring. If we are too rushed, over-stimulated, or too stressed out, the chances are that we will not be as altruistic, kind, and compassionate as we are built to be. Also, if we are wrapped up in our own problems, we tend to be more selfish. Goleman puts it this way:

> In short, self-absorption in all its forms kills empathy, let alone compassion. When we focus on ourselves, our world contracts as our problems and preoccupations loom large. But when we focus on others, our world expands. Our own problems drift to the periphery of the mind and so seem smaller, and we increase our capacity for connection — or compassionate action.

So, despite what the 11 o'clock news and the collective media would have you believe, we are generally a loving, kind, compassionate, and altruistic species. Yes, we can be apathetic, cold, calculating, and violent in words and deeds, but on any given day, these feelings and behaviors occur much less often than caring and kind acts.

I find this somewhat comforting. We're not so bad after all. We may have bad days when we're nowhere near the top of our game, but basically, we're a decent bunch. Life is challenging, and we can make it easier for ourselves and for each other simply by manifesting our biological hardwiring towards altruism. I'll try to do my part. Think of the ramifications if we all hold up our end of the bargain. Remember, it's contagious. Catch it!

I'LL NEVER LEAVE YOU

It was somewhere between mile number 22 and mile number 23 of the Alaska Marathon. Only about three and a half miles to go. I felt good — probably as good as anyone can feel after running 22 and a half miles. I was approaching two runners, one of whom was obviously hurting. As I got closer, I ran behind them for a bit, listening to their animated conversation. The guy who was struggling was telling the other guy to go ahead without him. The other guy wouldn't hear of it.

"I'll never leave you. We're going to finish this thing together. You can do it! Just stay with me!"

The hurting guy answered, "I can't do it. I've got nothing left. You go. Don't worry about me."

The reply was, "Never. It's you and me the whole way. You and me together. 'Til the end. Come on. Keep it going!"

They went back and forth like this a few more times. I thought to myself about that kind of deep friendship where you're committed to helping a friend no matter what. I wondered if they might be brothers or be related through blood or school or work or community. In any event, I felt confident that their bond was enduring and admirable. As I was passing them, I heard the one guy say to the other, "Hey, what did you say your name was?"

This story could illustrate a number of things. It could be about acts of kindness, camaraderie, or needing others while in the midst of a struggle. Or maybe it's more about finding friendship and what it takes to be a friend. Many studies on happiness have shown that friendships are highly correlated with life satisfaction. If you have good friends, consider yourself blessed. Nurture those friendships. If you are lacking good friends, it's worth your while to open yourself up to the possibility of starting a new friendship. Reach out. The next one may be a keeper. It's never too late to make a friend, even if you're at the 23-mile mark of the marathon.

IF YOU WANT TO BE HAPPY FOR THE REST OF YOUR LIFE...

There was a song in the 1960s that had the refrain, "If you want to be happy for the rest of your life, never make a pretty woman your wife...." I honestly don't think that's the answer to finding everlasting happiness, but the following anecdote might put you on the right path:

> A venerable old sage was meeting with a student for the final time. The eager student was ready to get the final and most important teaching of the wise guru. He leaned forward. The teacher whispered in his ear, "Be a good person."

In Yiddish, the world "mensch" means just being a decent human being in all respects—a down-to-earth, ordinary human being who's kind to others and lives by the golden rule or something that resembles it. He's not arrogant or smug, doesn't feel entitled, and is more likely to count his blessings than his money. A mensch is responsible, has integrity, and has a keen sense of what's right and what's wrong. There's an old saying, "I wouldn't touch that with a ten-foot pole." Well, a mensch wouldn't touch it with a 20-foot pole.

A mensch doesn't think he's better than anyone else and is the kind of person you'd want for a friend. You know you can trust him with your life. He's what's known as a "stand-up guy."

You know a mensch. She's non-judgmental and maybe a pinch self-effacing. She's not interested in being powerful or famous. She'd go out of her way to help you. You can count on her. She's fair, kind, loving, compassionate, and concerned. You feel fortunate to know her. Every mensch makes the world a bit better.

I can't vouch for never making a pretty woman your wife or a handsome man your husband leading to a life of happiness, but I'm pretty certain that being a mensch greatly improves your chances. Sonja Lyubomirsky is a professor of psychology at the University of California. She has shown through her research that practicing five acts of kindness a day produces ongoing happiness. Doing kind things for friends, family, or strangers (even anonymously), whether planned or spontaneous, helps create happiness.

In the book and movie *Pay It Forward*, a 12-year-old boy named Trevor tells his mother and teacher of an idea he has:

> You see, I do something real good for three people. And then when they ask how they can pay it back, I say they have

to pay it forward. To three more people.
Each. So nine people get helped. Then
those people have to do 27.

(He takes out a calculator and punches in
a few numbers.)

Then it sort of spreads out, see. To 81.
Then 243. Then 729. Then 2,187. See how
big it gets?

Next time someone does something nice for you, even if you
pay it back, consider paying it forward.

A RAINY DAY

I got up early today to continue working on this book. This is exactly what I want to be doing. It's work, but it's play. I'm on summer vacation in Cape Cod. Usually, I do my writing in a shady area of the backyard, surrounded by trees I planted 20 years ago. But today is monsoon-like with torrential rain and high winds. So today, I'm sitting at the kitchen table, alternating my attention between writing and peering out the window.

As an adult, I've always loved watching the rain. If I'm lucky enough to be able to sit outside on a porch, I'll take a cup of tea with me to enjoy while I watch. I hold the cup to my face and let the steam soothe my eyes. Some of my favorite memories include doing this during the cold autumns in the mountains of Pennsylvania. On the porch, under blankets, watching the driving rain while sipping tea. But today, it's the summer rain from the kitchen window.

My wife is asleep. So is my son. My daughter, too. It's early.

I feel blessed. I'm thankful for a million things. At least. That I'm alive, for starters. I didn't imagine I would reach this age. It all seems like gravy to me. I'm thankful that I'm surrounded by family and that I have all my faculties so I'm able to write. I'm thankful I'm not in pain and that I don't have any debilitating conditions or diseases. I'm thankful for all the things that I don't have that I don't want. And I'm thankful for all the people that make my life meaningful and loving: my wife and children and family and friends and patients.

As I take a break to gaze at the rain, my eyes are drawn to the Black-eyed Susans. Despite the bleak weather and without the aid of sunshine, their color still lights up the view framed by the kitchen window. And despite the fury of the winds, they keep popping up again and again. Yes, it's one of those mornings that I'm seemingly more grateful than usual (and I'm usually very grateful) for no apparent reason. I often feel this way when I don't hurry through life and when I stop to think about everything that goes right throughout the day — the little things and big things I may take for granted. I guess I feel this way when I stop to look around. Mary Oliver, one of my favorite poets, suggests that we should never hurry through life and that we should walk slowly and bow often.

WHAT ARE YOU WAITING FOR?

Being kind, loving, and generous greatly enhances your chances of being happier. How do you measure up on these dimensions? I'm less interested in your good intentions and more concerned with what you do and say—how you actually lead your life. There is no truth except in action.

Harvard students are asked to do something very pleasurable such as engage in sex, eat a delicious meal, go skiing, see a concert or movie, and so on. They're also asked to do something altruistic such as a random act of kindness, volunteering for charitable work, or helping at a soup kitchen. Overwhelmingly, they feel happier in connection to the altruistic act than they do with regard to the pleasurable act.

Giving of yourself makes sense. It's a win-win proposal. It works for everyone. Being kind and loving and manifesting a sincere generosity of spirit will indeed help you to feel happier. And it doesn't cost you a thing.

In *A Christmas Carol*, the miser, Ebeneezer Scrooge, learns from the spirits of the past, present, and future. The lesson is that it's important to be generous with money and even more important to be generous with love and kindness. He is given a second chance and we see the crotchety, old, "Bah Humbug!" tightwad morph into the happy, giving, young-at-heart, warm Uncle Ebeneezer and savior of Tiny Tim.

Yes, it's never too late to be a kinder person. It's contagious. Being kind will lift your spirits as well as the spirits of the recipients of your kindness. Being kind is, in fact, a holy act if you put it in the context of religion or spirituality. But aside from that context, kindness anytime under any circumstances is worthwhile and is its own reward. Can you imagine if everyone were kinder? In your house, neighborhood, town, state, country, and throughout the world? Let it start with you. Sylvia Boorstein puts it this way:

> Becoming aware of fragility, of temporality, of the fact that we will surely be lost to one another, sooner or later, mandates a clear imperative to be totally kind and loving to each other always. People sometimes say about a critically ill person, "Her days are numbered." All of our days are numbered. No one knows what number we are up to. Literally, we haven't a moment to lose.

Be kind whenever possible.
It's always possible.
–Dalai Lama

COFFEE WITH MILK

Pardon me if I'm repeating myself or if it seems like I'm hitting you over the head with a hammer. This bears repeating. I want you to get it. Gratitude and appreciation are the keys to genuine and meaningful happiness. Again and again it has been demonstrated that happy people focus more on what they have while unhappy people are preoccupied with what they perceive they don't have. Happier people tend to do that old-fashioned thing of counting their blessings. Less-than-happy people are more self-absorbed and tend to see problems in their lives wherever they look. Jon Gordon offers the following advice:

> When the work is piled high on your desk,
> think about how thankful you are to even
> have a job while so many are unemployed.
> When work is driving you crazy, think
> about the fact you are healthy enough

to work. When you are sitting in traffic, be thankful you can drive a car while so many have to walk miles just to get clean water. When the restaurant messes up your meal, think about how many unfed mouths there are in the world.

Dr. Michael McCollough and Dr. Robert Emmons are psychologists who researched the effects of gratitude. Their study divided hundreds of people into three different groups. Everyone kept a daily diary. The members of group number one simply documented the events of the day. Group two members only recorded their unpleasant experiences. Each day, the individuals of the third group listed things they were grateful for. Results from the study showed that the group three members experienced less stress and less depression. They were more likely to be enthusiastic, optimistic, helpful to others, and made more progress toward personal goals. Expressing their gratitude seemed to encourage a positive cycle of reciprocal kindness. Martin Seligman advises the following:

> ...think back over the previous twenty-four hours and write down, on separate lines, up to five things in your life you are grateful or thankful for. Common examples include "waking up this morning," "the generosity of friends," "God for giving me determination," "wonderful parents," "robust good health," and "The Rolling Stones" (or some other artistic inspiration).

You can learn to feel more gratitude and appreciation by doing this daily. Start paying attention to all you have to be appreciative of. It will add immensely to the quality of your life. Please digest the poem "Coffee With Milk" by Natalie Goldberg:

It is very deep to have a cup of tea
Also coffee in a white cup
With milk
A hand to go around the cup
And a mouth to open and take it in
It is very deep and very good to have a heart
Do not take the heart for granted
It fills with blood and lets blood out

Good to have this chair to sit in
With these feet on the floor
While I drink this coffee
In a white cup
To have the air around us to be in
To fill our lungs and empty them like weeping
This roof to house us
The sky to house the roof in endless blue
To be in the Midwest
With the Atlantic over there
And the Pacific on our other side

It is good this cup of coffee
The milk in it
The cows who gave us this milk
This
Simple as a long piece of grass

Dance on the edge of mystery.
–Alan Cohen

VI.
FAITH
&
MYSTERY

I would believe only in a God
that knows how to dance.
–Friedrich Nietzsche

WOULD YOU LIKE FRIES WITH THAT?

To be happy, it is essential that you find meaning in life. To feel connected to something larger and more permanent than yourself such as religion, nature, or a belief system provides purpose and a sense of well-being. Many, if not most people, place their faith in spirituality or religion as a way of finding comfort and meaning as well as possibly finding a way to deal with the omnipresent issue of mortality. My brother Sam, a disabled veteran of the Korean War, used to say, "You don't find an atheist in a foxhole." It is true that people become more religious in times of crisis. When we are frightened, traumatized, or grieving, we need to find a way to continue having faith. This faith sustains us in our most difficult times.

Studies indicate that in the United States, over 90 percent of the people believe in a personal God. In fact, we may be hardwired to believe in religion. Writing in *The New York Times*, Robin Marantz Henig states:

Angels, demons, spirits, wizards, gods and witches have peppered folk religions since mankind first started telling stories. Charles Darwin noted this in *The Descent of Man*. "A belief in all-pervading spiritual agencies," he wrote, "seems to be universal." According to anthropologists, religions that share certain supernatural features—belief in a non-corporeal God or gods, belief in the afterlife, belief in the ability of prayer or ritual to change the course of human events—are found in virtually every culture on earth.

If religion has helped us to endure and survive, this evolutionary phenomenon has most likely produced a physical brain that makes it easier for us to find and/or believe in religion when we need it most. Our perceptions are greatly influenced by our wants and needs. It isn't "seeing is believing" as much as it is "believing is seeing."

Diane Duyser was about to bite into her grilled cheese sandwich when she saw the Virgin Mary staring back at her. After keeping the toast in a plastic box for a decade, she sold it on an eBay auction for $28,000. Evidently, the toast did not mold or decompose in those ten years. Ms. Duyser considers it a miracle and claims she won $70,000 in a casino because of it.

Cruz Jacinto, a kitchen worker in California, was struggling with life and was losing faith in her religion. She was questioning the existence of God when she discovered a two-inch lump of chocolate bearing the Virgin Mary's likeness. Her faith was restored and the chocolate now rests in a display case where people pray and place rose petals and candles around it.

When they opened a packet of Rold Gold Honey Mustard Pretzels in their Nebraska home, the Naylor family discovered a pretzel that looked like the Virgin Mary. It was placed for auction on the Internet. Recently, on Ash Wednesday, an elementary school kitchen worker in Texas discovered a grease stain on a pizza pan that bore the silhouette of the Virgin Mary. A shrine was erected for the pizza pan. As I'm working on this story, a new sighting has taken place. The Virgin Mary has appeared to an Arizona family on a slice of watermelon.

A brief look at Jesus sightings includes Jesus on a shrimp tail, on a pierogi, on a fish bone, in the overspill of a hot chocolate, and in a tortilla. Thousands of people made pilgrimages to view the tortilla and prayed for help to cure their ailments. The word "pareidolia" is of Greek origin. Para means faulty and eidolon means image. Religious pareidolia is the term for when we look at an ambiguous stimulus and see something involving religious themes that are very specific and important, or even miraculous.

Examples of these phenomena are legion, and not only in Christianity. Among Muslims, perceiving the word "Allah" on foods has been widely reported. A chicken in a Kazakhstan village laid an egg with the word "Allah" inscribed on its shell. The farmer, Bites Amantayeva, said, "We'll keep this egg and we don't think it will go bad." "Allah" has also been seen on beans, tomatoes, fish, vegetables, and a newborn lamb.

In Thailand, when it was reported that a puddle formed in the shape of Buddha's footprints, thousands of people came to see it and believed it to be a holy place. It was thought that the puddle of water could relieve suffering and bring good luck to those who visited.

Recently, when Gary Marcus was unemployed, his wife,

Marsha, contacted a rabbi to seek his help. Rabbi Joshua Gordon sent an email blessing to them. Three days later, Gary yelled to Marsha to come into the kitchen and invoked her to bring a camera. In the pot of simmering oatmeal that Gary was cooking on the stove, the Star of David (which always had special meaning and a protective belief for Marsha) had formed. Marsha believed it to be a miracle.

Big Bang or Garden of Eden or both? In some respects, it doesn't seem to matter. We are creatures whose physiology and psychology have been shaped to keep us going. Unlike the dinosaurs, we are survivors. What enables us to not only survive, but also to coexist with the knowledge of our eventual deaths—as well as the deaths of everyone we love? And how can we be happy in spite of all this? It seems that we need to transcend our own mortality by our belief in something larger and more permanent than ourselves. Anyone interested in taking a leap of faith?

CHOPSTICKS

A young Zen student was unexpectedly taken seriously ill. After several days, he realized that he would not survive his illness. Lying on his deathbed, he requested that his chopsticks be brought to him. Upon hearing this request, his master came to his room and stood staring at him, not knowing what to say.

"My request surprises you, doesn't it?" the student asked.

"Yes, I'm puzzled by your request," replied the master.

The young student explained, "My grandmother once told me that in all her years of sharing meals with others, she remembered that when the bowls of the main course were being cleared, someone would inevitably lean over and say, 'Keep your chopsticks.' It was her favorite part because she knew that something better was coming, like rice pudding or sweet fruits.

Something wonderful! Holding my chopsticks reminds me that 'the best is yet to come.'"

The master's eyes welled up with tears of joy as he hugged his young student goodbye. He knew this would be the last time he would see the student before his death. He also knew that the young student grasped the meaning of death as well as life.

You need a busload of faith to get by.
–Lou Reed

BECAUSE I CAN'T

Eleanor Arroway's mother died in childbirth. She was raised by her father, who helped her develop her interest in studying nebulae, quasars, and pulsars. By age eight, she was passionate about becoming an astronomer. When Eleanor was nine, her father died, but she pursued her dream and received her doctorate in astronomy. She always hoped to contact extraterrestrials. Other scientists laughed at her work, believing it to be science fiction rather than science. She was shunned. Her response was, "If I have to go it alone, I'll go it alone. I've done it before."

When Dr. Arroway received a message from Vega (a star), the SETI program (Search for Extraterrestrial Intelligence) was taken more seriously. A third of a trillion dollars was invested to build a spacecraft that would travel to Vega. Because she told the truth that she didn't think there was enough evidence to prove the existence of God, she was not chosen to go in the spacecraft to Vega. However, when a security breach compromised the mission and an explosion damaged the craft and killed the scientist on board, Dr. Arroway got to go on a second spacecraft that had been built simultaneously.

Here's where the plot thickens. She arrived on Vega and was greeted by her father. He told her:

> You're an interesting species, an interest-
> ing mix. You're capable of such beautiful
> dreams and such horrible nightmares.

and

> ... in all our searching, the only thing we
> found that makes the emptiness bearable
> is each other.

The hundreds of people working at the space center control area told Dr. Arroway that there was a malfunction and that her spacecraft never left the space center. They told her that she did not go to Vega and that all the scientific instruments confirmed that nothing happened. She stuck to her story.

A panel of investigators convened to question her in front of a packed courtroom. They wanted her to admit that she "suffered some kind of episode" and was delusional. The main investigator of the congressional committee assertively asked, "Are you really going to sit there and tell us we should just take this all on faith?" When she admitted having no physical evidence to support her story, the investigator queried, "Then why don't you simply withdraw your testimony and concede that this journey to the center of the galaxy in fact never took place?"

Dr. Arroway replied, "Because I can't." She went on. "I had

an experience. I can't prove it. I can't even explain it … it was real. I was given a vision that tells us that we belong to something that is greater than ourselves, that none of us are alone. I wish that everyone, if even for a moment, could feel that awe and humility and hope." She added, "The universe is a pretty big place. If it's just us, it seems like an awful waste of space." Science, mystery, religion, and faith can make strange bedfellows. Einstein, the most brilliant scientist of all, summarized his own beliefs on the matter:

> The most beautiful emotion we can experience is the mysterious. It is the fundamental emotion that stands at the cradle of all true art and science. He to whom this emotion is a stranger, who can no longer wonder and stand rapt in awe, is as good as dead, a snuffed-out candle. To sense that behind anything that can be experienced there is something that our minds cannot grasp, whose beauty and sublimity reaches us only indirectly: this is religiousness. In this sense, and in this sense only, I am a devoutly religious man.

To paraphrase Joseph Campbell, Eleanor Arroway followed her bliss. When others doubted her and laughed at her, she remained open-minded and optimistic. She evidenced a keen sense of curiosity and interest in the world. She persevered despite feeling discouraged at times. She remained hopeful. Dr. Arroway trusted herself. Despite not being a deeply religious person, she felt a connection to something larger than herself, whether you want to label it the soul, the spirit, God, nature, the cosmos, or the force. When the congressional pressure mounted on her to change her story, she ultimately trusted herself, deciding that her own experience should be a higher authority than the critical voices of her detractors. It would have been easy to recant her testimony, but she'd have none of it. She evidenced courage and integrity. Dr. Arroway was a living primer on the ingredients that are important for happiness.

Due to the malfunction of her spacecraft, the control center said that she had only been in the cockpit for a minute and therefore never got to Vega. Dr. Arroway argued that her mission lasted 18 hours. It was later discovered that the video camera in her spacecraft had 18 hours of static on it. A minute or so on earth would be the equivalent of about 18 hours in light years. Hmmmmm.

UZBEKISTAN

I recently mentioned to my wife, Nan, that I think you can buy cars with heated seats. She broke into hysterical laughter. When she composed herself, she said to me, "Where are you from? Uzbekistan?" Evidently, heated seats in cars have been available for at least 20 years. Not only did I not know that, I had no idea where Uzbekistan was. I decided to look it up.

Just in case you don't know, Uzbekistan is a region of ancient cities along the Silk Road trading route between China and the West. Samarkand, one of the oldest cities in the world, is in this area. Such infamous names as Attila the Hun and Genghis Khan are associated with that region.

I guess when Nan asked me if I was from Uzbekistan, it was her way of saying I can be a bit behind modern times. It's true. Guilty as charged. Not only did I not know of heated seats, I have to admit I've never seen an episode of Law and Order or Desperate Housewives. I've never had a massage or caller ID.

I'm technologically challenged, entertainment-world challenged, latest-fashion challenged, and 21st-century challenged. Yes, I may be a bit behind the times, but I'm content.

> Albert Einstein's wife often suggested that he dress more professionally when he headed off to work. "Why should I?" he would invariably argue. "Everyone knows me there." When the time came for Einstein to attend his first major conference, she begged him to dress up a bit. "Why should I?" said Einstein. "No one knows me there!"

Here's the thing: I think it's fine not to know everything. I find that with each passing year, I feel the need to know less and less rather than more and more. Not knowing about heated car seats or where Uzbekistan is doesn't interfere with my life or with my happiness. I think my brain only holds a certain amount of information anyhow. And the more that I know, it confirms that I really know less, and that the world is indeed filled with mystery.

Steven Wright said, "You can't have everything. Where would you put it?"

My corollary is, "You can't know everything. Where would you put it?" I'm pretty sure I don't have the definitive answers to life's big questions such as:

> –What is the meaning of life?
> –What happens when you die?
> –Why did the chicken cross the road?

I don't think happiness is related to having all the answers. In that regard, I like the quote of Rachel Naomi Remen:

> Perhaps real wisdom lies in not seeking answers at all. Any answer we find will not be true for long. An answer is a place where we can fall asleep as life moves past us to its next question. After all these years, I have begun to wonder if the secret of living well is not in having all the answers but in pursuing unanswerable questions in good company.

THE GAIA HYPOTHESIS

Brooks Atkinson once said, "I have no objection to churches so long as they do not interfere with God's work." I agree. I believe that religion can be a wonderful thing, but it can also be divisive, narrow-minded, inflexible, and the cause of Holy Wars, just to name a few possibilities. Recently, a friend of mine who had been a devoted member of her church her entire life was scolded by her orthodox priest for taking communion at a non-orthodox church she was visiting. I've heard similar stories from people of all faiths about their dealings with their rabbis, priests, ministers, senseis, and other teachers and clergy.

> A donkey with a load of
> holy books is still a donkey.
> (Sufi Wisdom)

Research scientist Dr. James Lovelock formulated the Gaia

Hypothesis in the 1960s. It was named after the Greek earth goddess Gaia and stemmed from the work he was doing for NASA. The hypothesis formulates that our planet is a single living organism that continually regulates itself to maintain homeostasis and biochemical balance. In *1001 Pearls of Wisdom*, David Ross elaborates:

> The earth is likened to a body: its oceans and rivers are its blood vessels and the atmosphere is its lungs. Personifying the earth in this way, as a cosmic being, makes it seem automatically more sacred.

One way of interpreting the Gaia hypothesis is that you are the universe and everything and everyone in it, and that the universe is you. One big organism. Brad Warner writes of an enlightening experience he had not long after completing a meditation retreat:

> Even if I want to put this realization down, I can't. Sometimes it's excruciating. You know those morons that rammed those planes into the World Trade Center? That was me. The people that died in the collapse. Me again. Every single person who ever paid money for a Pet Rock? Me. I don't mean I identify with them or sympathize with them. I mean I am them. It's impossible to explain any more clearly than that, but this isn't a figure of speech or bad poetry. I mean it absolutely literally.

But the universe is sooooo much bigger than any of that.

The sky is me, and the stars too, and the chirping crickets and the songs they make; sparkling rivers, snow and rain, distant solar systems and whatever beings may live there: it's all me. And it's you, too.

At the very least, I find the Gaia Hypothesis quite interesting. I'm ambivalent about being the same organism as rapists, child molesters, and so on. I guess if an individual can develop cancerous cells and gross anomalies and aberrations, so can the planet. Maybe the terrorists, molesters, and rapists are like mutant cells. As individuals, we recognize that we don't feel well all of the time and sometimes make poor choices. I guess some days we are just out of kilter. You can probably apply that to the planet as well. Hey, one all-encompassing single organism isn't always on the top of its game either.

Someone once said, "Wherever I look I see the face of God." That's more the point for me. When we can shed the restrictions that come with the labels of Jew, Catholic, Protestant, Muslim, Buddhist, Hindu, and so on, we can experience the oneness of the universe and transform how we perceive the world. If we don't divide the world into labels such as Asia, Europe, Antarctica, outer space, oceans, you, me, him, them, us, it, and so on, we can see the world as being one huge organism.

It's easy to see yourself as a separate living organism with your own heart, blood supply, organs, bones, muscles, brain, and body. What if we saw the entire world that way, as just one big organism with everyone and everything being interconnected? If that were the case, how could anyone treat anyone poorly? It would be like shooting yourself in the foot.

> One day while editing a transcription of
> Suzuki Roshi's first lecture on the San-
> dokai, I came upon the phrase "things as
> it is." I asked him if perhaps he had not
> meant to say "things as they are," which
> I thought to be proper syntax. "No," he
> said, "what I meant is 'things as it is.'"
> –*Zen Is Right Here*

A DIME STORE MYSTERY

I'm ruminating on a Lou Reed song called "Dime Store Mystery":

> I know the feeling, I know it from before
> Descartes through Hegel belief is never sure
> Dime store mystery ....

> I was sitting drumming thinking thumping pondering
> The mysteries of life
> Outside the city shrieking screaming whispering
> The mysteries of life

Ah, life—mysterious life. We like to think it's all about predictability, control, security, and black and white explanations. Ha. Science doesn't have all the answers and probably never will. Technology and sophisticated research can't measure or quantify all of our experiences. Neither can religion. Things happen that are beyond explanation. They just do. Hasn't something like that happened to you? Usually, we're too frightened or embarrassed to open ourselves fully to these happenings. We believe most people would think less of us for having them. We think they would discount our experience, see it as some unworthy dime store mystery.

In *Travels With Charley*, John Steinbeck drives across America to find out about its people and himself:

> The night was loaded with omens. The grieving sky turned the little water to a dangerous metal and then the wind got up—not the gusty, rabbity wind of the seacoasts I know but a great bursting sweep of wind with nothing to inhibit it for a thousand miles in any direction. Because it was a wind strange to me, and therefore mysterious, it set up mysterious responses in me. In terms of reason, it was strange only because I found it so. But a goodly part of our experience which we find inexplicable must be like that. To my certain knowledge, many people conceal experiences for fear of ridicule. How many people have seen or heard or felt something which so outraged their sense of what should be that the whole thing was brushed quickly away like dirt under a rug? For myself, I try to keep the line open even for things I can't under-

stand or explain, but it is difficult in this frightened time.

The mystery manifests itself in a variety of ways. It's not only available to yogis, clergy, gurus, and new age seekers. In fact, Meredith Jordan has written a beautiful book called *Embracing the Mystery: The Sacred Unfolding in Ordinary People and Everyday Lives*. Yes, ordinary people and everyday lives. That's you and me and him and her and them. Mystery can be frightening, but it can also bring joy, purpose, meaning, and astonishment. Have you considered opening up to the mysteries you've experienced? Getting a glimpse of the mysterious doesn't mean you are not a sane and rational person.

> Everybody has his or her own possibility of rapture in the experience of life. All one has to do is to recognize it and then cultivate it and get going with it.... It's important to live life with the experience, and therefore the knowledge, of its mystery and your own mystery. This gives life a new radiance, a new harmony, a new splendor. The big question is whether you are going to be able to say a hearty yes to your own adventure.
> –Joseph Campbell, *The Power of Myth*

VII.
TAKE IT ALL IN

Dance with everything.

BUILDING ROME

To say that patience is a virtue is accurate but is also an understatement. Patience is one of the most important traits to cultivate. We are an impatient society. We like things done yesterday. We are impatient with ourselves and with others. We value multitasking and pride ourselves on how quickly we can get things done. We eat fast food, and we eat it too quickly. We're impatient when we have to wait in lines or get caught in traffic jams. When we're impatient, our minds and bodies tense and a cascade of chemical reactions is set into effect. We're more likely to say things we regret and make impulsive decisions. Our health suffers. Relationships suffer. Impatience breeds hostility, frustration, and aggravation.

My advice would be to slow down, breathe deeply, and practice letting go of your impatience.

As he neared a grove of trees, the apprentice monk met Buddha. Buddha smiled and took his hand. They went to a temple where two old monks were sweeping the floor. Buddha said to them, "This young monk will live here with you. Continue sweeping, and as your brooms move back and forth, listen carefully to the sounds they make. Don't stop until I come back."

The young monk sat down and listened to the movement of the brooms, to and fro over the floor. The sweeping sounds repeated over and over again. Just this. It went on for many weeks, and before Buddha returned, the young monk and the two old monks were enlightened.

–Majjhima Nikaya

Aesop said that "slow and steady wins the race." Does there even have to be a race? It's also been said that "haste makes waste." I believe that. We're a high-tech society always looking for faster this and faster that. It's not always in our best interest. Practice patience. Be patient with yourself and others and with your practice.

The martial arts student said to the venerable teacher, "I am devoted to studying. How long will it take me to master the martial arts?"

The teacher replied, "Ten years."

Impatiently, the student responded, "That's too long. I want to master it faster than that. I'll practice fourteen hours a day. It will consume me. Now, how long would it take me?"

The teacher replied, "Twenty years."

DELAYING GRATIFICATION

Many moons ago, when I was a fledgling psychotherapist growing up in the counter culture movement of the 1960s and 1970s, a great premium was placed on getting patients to be spontaneous. They were urged to "let it all hang out," "go with the flow," and to stop thinking and just express their feelings. That was the era of encounter groups, Esalan, and primal scream therapy. That, my friends, was a long time ago.

Spontaneity is not necessarily a good thing. In fact, it can get a person in big trouble. It can also cause a lot of pain for others. Don't say everything you think. Don't express everything you feel as you feel it. The value of being spontaneous is overrated. The new mantra is "patience." Recently, a professor having a few months left to live gave his last lecture. He passed on his near-death bed wisdom to a packed audience. It included, "Be patient with others."

You might get a measure of gratification from expressing

your frustration, envy, anger, sarcasm, and the like. You might satisfy some needs temporarily by spontaneously overeating, drinking too much, or overspending. The likelihood is your pleasure will be short-lived. A hallmark characteristic of maturity and self-esteem is the ability to delay gratification in favor of long range goals and benefits. It is not in your best interest to say anything you feel like, and it's not healthy to get everything that you want when you want it. Be patient with yourself and with others. It will make a big difference.

> When Albert Einstein and his wife, Mileva, were having serious marital problems, Einstein proposed a deal. He had little money at the time, but he told Mileva that someday he would win the Nobel Prize. If she agreed to divorce him, he would give her the substantial prize money that came with the award. She thought about the proposal for a week. She accepted. Einstein's theories were so radical that it took a long time for the Nobel Prize judges to honor him. Seventeen years after their agreement, Mileva collected her money.

JIBBER JABBER

Are you by yourself? Shut off the TV. The radio, too. Forget about CD, MP3, DVD, and Blu-ray players. Turn off your iPhone or BlackBerry or Droid or any other cell phone. Your computer, too. Forget about all electronic devices and gadgets that you are enamored with. Don't clean or organize anything. No crossword puzzles, jumbles, Sudoku, magazines, or newspapers. I want you to try something. Without anything to distract you, just sit by yourself for 15 minutes. I'm serious. Put this book down now and just sit by yourself with nothing to distract you. Come back to this story in 15 minutes.

What was that like for you? The reason I asked you to do that is because many emotional problems are the result of not being able to sit quietly without creating anxiety or unhappiness.

Sitting quietly, doing nothing,
Spring comes and grass grows of itself.
–Zenrin Kushu

In my book *Seven Times Down, Eight Times Up*, there was a story called "Yada Yada Yada." In my book *The Happiness Solution*, there was one called "Blah Blah Blah." They had to do with the ceaseless chatter that goes on in our minds and complicates our lives. This chatter, or self-babble, focuses on everything that we can conjure up to convince ourselves that we're not enough, what we have isn't enough, that others have what we want, and that the future is fraught with perils and problems. This chatter tells us that we've been shortchanged in our relationships and that life isn't particularly fair. These are just a few examples of the type of self-chatter that we indulge in. Recently, a patient of mine referred to this as "jibber jabber." Prattle, gibber, gabble, tittle-tattle, yakety yak, or self-blabber might be other ways of labeling this phenomenon. Any name you want to call it, it's the equivalent of hitting your head against the wall—painful and unconstructive.

If you are able to sit quietly with yourself and feel good, congratulations. That is wonderful. It is like being a good friend to yourself and enjoying the company that you keep, even when you are alone. If you had problems with this experiment, or if you know that your jibber jabber leaves you feeling down or on edge, please read the next story and give it a try.

DON'T DO SOMETHING, JUST SIT THERE

Take 5 or 10 minutes a day to sit and do nothing. Okay, you can do it for 15 to 20 minutes if you'd like. This isn't as easy as it sounds. Many people feel uncomfortable sitting still, doing nothing. Some feel guilt. Others feel anxiety. If you get comfortable with sitting and doing nothing, it can be life-changing.

Find some privacy, sit in a chair, and close your eyes. Take gentle breaths originating below your navel. Just breathing in slowly. Just breathing out slowly. Focus on your breathing. When thoughts arise, simply let them go and return your awareness to your breathing. Treat every thought the same, no matter what it is. Let it go and shift your focus to your breathing. Just do this continually. It's as if you're just an observer. You're not sitting in judgment. You're not evaluating. You're like an impartial witness of the process. Just breathing in slowly and just breathing out slowly. That's all there is to it. Try it. The benefits are cumulative. Keep it going.

This is a process of learning how to befriend yourself and how not to give yourself a hard time. You learn not to cling to thoughts and not to believe everything you think. So, when you don't know what to do with yourself, don't do anything—just sit there.

TAKE IT ALL IN

In her poem titled "Spring," Darryl Anne Burnham reminds us to "Look around. Really look." She also reminds us to "Take it all in." Wonderful advice from a 10-year-old girl. How many of us take the time to do it—to really look? Can we stop hurrying and scurrying long enough to truly take in and appreciate the wonder, awe, and mystery of nature and life? Slow down. Breathe deeply. It's important that you do. The quality of your life depends on it.

Spring

Look around.
Really look.
See the last bit of sky,
The sun setting on the tree tops.
Hear the birds sing their last song.
Listen to the stream flowing.

It could sing you right off to sleep.
Feel the cool wind in your face.
The wind is cool but the air is warm.
See the stillness of the night.
It is magnificent.
The wind is starting to blow.
Take it all in.

You can hear the last of the birds call.
It is almost as if they are saying,
"It's getting dark, better go in."
"No."
You want to stay out just a bit longer.
You can't seem to get enough of the cool, still night.
Take one last look.
Look at this beautiful place before you go in.
It really is lovely.
You think to yourself,
"This must be a true spring."
Gather it all in.

You feel free.
You are free.

Very shortly after writing this poem, Darryl, a beautiful, vibrant, and loving child, unexpectedly died at age 10. I think of her daily. I look around. I really look. How about you? As Darryl reminds you in the last line of her poem, "You are free." Take it all in.

[Please see notes on page 275.]

FASTER HORSES

In *The Best Buddhist Writing: 2004*, Daizui MacPhillamy discusses what he calls the "faster horses problem." He relates the story of the young man who meets an old cowboy sitting in a bar. The young seeker of wisdom is certain that this old, weather-beaten cowboy knows the answers to life's important questions. He asks the old guy lots of questions about the meaning of life and what brings happiness. No matter what the youngster asks, the old cowboy gives the same answer: "Faster horses, younger lovers, older whiskey, and more money!" MacPhillamy uses this story to illustrate the root of most of humanity's problems: we're never satisfied. We dream of or chase after faster horses. And, as long as we're dreaming and chasing the faster horses that we believe are necessary for our happiness, we're dissatisfied with ourselves, our loved ones, and our lives.

There's nothing wrong with having goals and aspiring to reach them. And we all like to have pleasurable sensations.

But if we're never truly satisfied — if we always think we need more (power, prestige, fame, sex, love, conquests, possessions, money) — it will be virtually impossible to attain peace of mind, joy, and meaning. Wanting faster horses leads to fear, anxiety, worry, anger, regret, frustration, and unhappiness. The craving for things to be different than they are creates disenchantment with the way things are. There are two effective ways of dealing with this.

The first is meditation. Several of the previous stories have already suggested this. One of the basic instructions in learning how to meditate is to not be bluffed by thoughts or feelings. You are told to focus on your breathing. If you become aware of thoughts, you simply let go of them and shift your consciousness back to your breathing — again and again... and again. Every thought, regardless of its content, is treated exactly alike. You just let it go without fanfare. No indulgence of any thoughts or feelings. They're all treated the same. It's as if you are a nonjudgmental, dispassionate observer of your thoughts and feelings. You note them and move on, refocusing on your breathing. Months of practice will have you relating to yourself very differently. Now, when the faster horses show up in your mind, you can just observe them, let them go, and shift your attention.

The other effective way of dealing with the faster horses phenomenon is cognitive-behavioral therapy. This involves the recognition that your thoughts are creating problems for you, and learning to rethink situations, to produce more rational and reasonable thoughts, which in turn would lead to feeling and behaving differently. Now, when your mind produces an invitation for you to fall into the faster horses trap, you say, "No, thank you. I know a faster horse is not the answer. It would only be a very temporary solution. Then, I'd need an even faster horse than that. No, thank you. I don't need a faster horse." It's a very circuitous route to happiness, with detours and obstacles. The faster horses may not fare well on this terrain. Get a slower horse. Relax. Take your time. Look around. Breathe deeply and enjoy the ride.

VIII.
FEAR, COURAGE,
&
RESILIENCY

When the music changes, so does the dance.
−African Proverb

THE NATURE OF THE BEAST

I like the Gilda Radner line that seems to be a parsimonious synopsis of life:

It's always something....

It's true. Life presents many challenges. We don't get much of what we want and we seem to get much of what we don't want. Relationships are disappointing. Health issues inevitably turn up. Job and family stresses add to our burden. What are we to do? Here's what I do. I do the best I can. That's probably what you need to do too.

It's always something. Try not to take it too personally. Practice being more of an optimist. An optimist believes that the "bad" things are time-limited and context-limited. The pessimist believes that they are permanent. The pessimist credo is "this too shall not pass."

Part of optimism is getting in touch with our resilience. As I frequently say and write, "There is a reason that dinosaurs are extinct and we're not." What helps build the foundation for resiliency is a sense of belongingness or connectedness. Good friends, supportive family, community, and healthy rituals are the building blocks of that foundation and you are the glue or cement that holds it all together. If you trust that you'll be able to deal with whatever you're dealt, you'll feel less anxious, less discouraged, more empowered, and more secure.

It's always something. If we are to be happy, we need to coexist with what is while we do the best that we can with the circumstances that we're dealing with. And those circumstances will pass. You are a survivor. You are resilient. Yes, it's always something, but you're capable of handling it, learning from it, and moving on to happiness.

The obstacle is the path.
–Zen proverb

THE MILLROSE GAMES

For those of you who are unfamiliar with the world of track and field, the Millrose Games is the nation's premier indoor meet. It is held annually at Madison Square Garden in New York City and attracts athletes from all over the world. Recently, my friend Carl and I were fortunate enough to attend the 100th Millrose Games, which began in 1908.

I find the games to be a microcosm of life. Anything can happen during the 39 events (including many relays) that make up the Millrose. There are some outcomes that hold true to form and are quite predictable. But still, you never know. There are surprises, exciting finishes, flubs, disappointments, arguments, joys, and well, the whole gamut of emotions. Athletes sometimes get ill or injured and sometimes they drop the relay batons. It not only affects them, but their teammates, coaches, and fans. Emotions can run pretty high at these competitions.

The Millrose Games draws the biggest crowd of any indoor

meet in the world. Madison Square Garden fills to the brim and the tension is palpable. Not all athletes and teams can compete. After all, this is the most historic and prestigious indoor invitational track meet in the world. The key word in the preceding sentence is "invitational." Not everyone who wants to compete can. You have to be invited. In the early decades of the event, the games were formal. Men and women would dress to the nines. It was customary for the women to wear dressy hats. The race officials wore tuxedos. Although the dress code is casual now, the officials still wear tuxedos to help preserve the uniqueness and prestige of Millrose.

So it was that in 1966, my senior year in college, the Holy Cross freshman relay team did not get the invitation they were hoping for to compete in the Millrose Games. Organizers denied their entry because all the spots were filled with other teams. When circumstances changed, a spot was found for the Holy Cross team, but inadvertently, they were never told. As fate would have it, all four runners went to the games to watch the track meet. Sitting in various parts of Madison Square Garden, they began to read the official program. All of them were astonished to read that they were supposed to be participating in the relay event. Two of the runners had just finished eating large meals before coming to the Garden. Another of the runners had already run four miles in the morning and later ice skated for three hours in the afternoon. They found each other in the stands, borrowed uniforms and running shoes, and got themselves to the starting line in time for their relay race. And so, their dream and goal of running in the world-famous Millrose Games had come true.

Life can take some strange twists and turns and can be quite unpredictable. My wife, who's also a psychotherapist, frequently says to her clients, "Fasten your seatbelt!" I'm incessantly reminding people to just do the best that they're capable of doing, without any expectations. I tell them that they aren't as fragile as they think and will find a way to deal with whatever comes their way, whenever it comes. As teenagers, my lifelong friend Sal and I had a little blurb that we often cited:

> Sometimes you win
> and sometimes you lose.
> Sometimes you get rained out.
> Sometimes, you don't even
> get tickets for the game.
> But, you always dress for it.

So, don't get too discouraged. Keep your eyes open and your chin up and be ready. Your opportunity may be just around the corner. And, just a little side note: the Holy Cross freshman relay team of 1966 won their race at the Millrose Games.

JUST ANOTHER DAY AT THE RANCH

I'm on my way to deliver a lay sermon for summer services at the Unitarian Church. My topic would be the title of one of my books, *Seven Times Down, Eight Times Up: Landing on Your Feet in an Upside Down World*. Yesterday, my brother Rip wound up getting a quintuple (five) bypass. He was in intensive care, in pain, and not fully out of the woods. At the same time, my sister, Harriet, was in a different hospital getting a cardiac catheterization to determine whether she might need a pacemaker or bypass. Yup, just another day at the ranch.

I had already lost two brothers, my sister-in-law, and my mother in the preceding couple of years. In a few days, I'd get the biopsy result as to whether or not I had melanoma. I felt a little like the soldier in *Saving Private Ryan* that they were trying to get out alive because his siblings had already died in the war. As I drove to the church to give my talk, I didn't feel cursed or less fortunate than anyone else. These are the things that happen to everyone. Occasionally, they may come in bunches. Everyone will get their turn. When your turn comes, there will be pain and sorrow. That's part of it too. No escape. There's no getting around it. If we want the joy, the love, the ecstasy, the serenity, the excitement, the passion, the beauty, and the transcendent, we have to take the illnesses, rejections, disappointments, traumas, and deaths. Try not to envy others who seemingly have it all. Their turn may be just around the corner.

I'm reminded of the story about the student who approaches the Zen Master and asks, "If I reach enlightenment, will I no longer be subject to emotional pain?" The Master replies, "That is not enlightenment; that is death."

> Sometimes I lie awake at night and ask,
> "Why me?" Then a voice answers,
> "Nothing personal, your name
> just happened to come up."
> –Charles Schultz

Oscar Wilde said, "If you don't get everything you want, think of the things that you don't get that you don't want." It sounds strange, but when things are not breaking your way, try not to take it personally. The universe is manifesting itself. Try to maintain a sense of humor. Life is less about what happens to you than it is about what you make of what happens to you.

> Life. It's full of such sadness and sorrow,
> sometimes I think it's better not to be born
> at all! But how many people do you meet
> in a lifetime who were that lucky?
> –Yiddish saying

Paraphrasing Johann Wolfgang Van Goethe, we enjoy when we can and endure when we must. And then, we enjoy what we can again. The cycle continues and exemplifies our innate capacity to bounce back and recover. I delivered the sermon on *Seven Times Down, Eight Times Up*. We may have our moments. We may get knocked down. But we always get up and get cooking again. We choose life.

BEAUTY AND THE BEAST

Once upon a time, running at the brink of dawn through difficult mountain trails, I spotted a large blackish-gray animal that was either a wolf or a wild dog. Guided by my fear and adrenaline rush, I immediately sped up and changed direction. Running for my life, I looked over my left shoulder to see if he was gaining on me. While looking back, I tripped over some gnarled tree roots and fell head first into rocks and brush. As I lay there stunned and bleeding, I sensed that the beast was approaching and eager to tear me apart. I looked in its direction. Imagine my surprise when it was still in the exact same spot that I originally saw it.

Getting up slowly and even more slowly collecting my wits, I began to painfully walk in the direction of the wild animal. It remained still. Getting closer, it became clear that the beast was a boulder. I had created the beast in my mind and related to it as if it were real. My fear was real, but it was based on my fictional thoughts and perceptions. Reflecting upon the experience, it struck me how much fear we needlessly manufacture in our day-to-day lives, even when we don't encounter backwoods beasts. We create it. We insist it's real. Then, we fret, freeze, flee, fight, or flail.

When I did get to that boulder that I originally ran from, I was able to see it for what it was, rather than relate to it solely from my mind's projections. It was anything but frightening. In fact, in its own way, it was quite beautiful. It was covered with a vibrant, deep green moss, the color of which you don't see in stores but rather only in nature. Its time-worn character was manifested in a network of nooks, crannies, and crevices.

Of course, there is a time for everything, including a time to be afraid. But much of that time that we are fearful, there is no good reason to feel that way. We've all seen those optical illusions that change from one thing to another as we continue to look at them. A popular one often shown in general psychology textbooks shifts between your seeing either an hourglass or two people in profile. To a large extent, your mind creates your world. When you feel fearful, keep looking at the fear until it dissolves. Think about the wild beast that was ready to devour me, and think about the beauty of that majestic boulder. An old expression has it that beauty is in the eye of the beholder. So is fear.

JUST SAY NO

I was a month shy of getting my doctorate in psychology. It had been a rough year. My father died suddenly. I hadn't seen him for many months. He was in New Jersey and I was a couple of thousand miles away in Utah. I had to pass a handful of four-hour written exams in various areas of psychology. If I passed those, that entitled me to take another handful of four-hour oral exams, essentially being grilled by a panel of professors. While all of this was occurring, I was writing a doctoral dissertation and had to defend it in front of a different group of professors. At the same time, I began my job search, which hopefully would land me my first full-time post-doctoral job. This was a very stressful time in my life.

So here I was in my late twenties, having served two years in the army and on the brink of getting my Ph.D., and feeling a whole host of varied and conflicted feelings. There were still unanswered metaphysical questions amidst so many practical issues to deal with. I went to a party with my friend Rich. There were many drugs there. I experimented. And then it happened: I began hallucinating. There were visual and auditory hallucinations. Delusions were not far behind. All my perceptual processes were affected — sights, sounds, smells, touch. Everything was markedly different. I was very frightened.

Rich kept telling me that it was just a "bad trip." I wasn't so sure. I told him I was brain damaged. An hour later, I told him I was schizophrenic. He said, "You're getting better already. An hour ago you were brain damaged. Now, you're just schizophrenic." In fact, I did have a seemingly drug-induced, paranoid schizophrenia that shook me to my foundations. Fortunately, I had completed all the difficult tasks to put me in position to get my Ph.D. Now, the only question was whether I'd be able to regain any semblance of my normal functioning so as to be able to have a career as a psychologist. As the days passed, my hallucinations and delusions continued and I continued to feel disoriented, confused, scared, and anxious.

In an effort to clear my head and regain my sanity, I took a week off and backpacked through the Grand Canyon. At week's end, I was not a new man. I neither cleared my head nor regained my sanity. I was simply a very disturbed guy who had experienced the Grand Canyon. So much for the geographical cure.

I received a call from a psychiatrist who headed up the psychiatric ward of a hospital in Maine. He liked my resume and wanted me to come to Maine for an interview as soon as possible. Although I was still psychotic, I accepted his offer. After I arrived, we had dinner at a local restaurant while he put me through the job interview. He had a very full beard and long hair. As he asked me about my education and experience, he began to morph into Wolfman and started howling. I did all I could to hold on. A job interview is stressful enough, but when you're being interviewed by Wolfman, stress takes on a whole new dimension. And in this case, Wolfman was an eminent chief psychiatrist who was carefully scrutinizing and assessing my every word, action, and demeanor. For about an hour, he snarled, howled, and growled his questions as he transformed from human to wolf to semi-human to beast. I hung on by the proverbial thread. What's a schizophrenic to do? At the end of the interview, he offered me the job. So much for his diagnostic skills.

That day, so many years ago, when I entered the world of the mentally ill, was the last time I ever used a drug. I'm a quick learner. It took about six months for the flashbacks to stop and for me to become free of delusions and hallucinations. In the interim, I kept plugging away and kept meeting my day-to-day responsibilities. I always remind myself to do the best I can. Frequently, I'll say to myself, "If you're not doing the best you can, what are you doing?"

As the eternal optimist that I am rightly accused of being, and in constant search of that proverbial silver lining, I do believe that my drug-induced schizophrenia helped make me a better therapist and continues to remind me that fear makes the wolf bigger than he is.

WHO'S RUNNING THE SHOW?

The noted author Sylvia Boorstein was at a gathering of meditation teachers in which each of them took turns sharing how they were and what was happening in their lives. Here's her account:

> As I listened to all of us speaking in turn, I was struck by one particular thing. As people spoke, they said things like, "I'm pretty content" or "I'm doing all right" or "I'm pretty happy." And yet, we all told regular stories. People had regular lives with regular Sturm und Drang. People had relationship problems, problems with aging parents; someone's child had a very serious illness; someone else was dealing with a difficult kind of loss. And

yet everyone said some variation of "I'm pretty much all right" or "I'm pretty content." And it didn't mean that they weren't struggling with what was happening to them. It did not mean that they had transcended their stories and that they were fine because they felt no pain from them. They *were* struggling and often in quite a lot of pain and concern, but still, they were all right. I thought to myself as I looked around, "What we're all doing is we're all managing gracefully."

How are you managing? Give it some thought. We're all managing in some way. Are you managing angrily? How about fearfully? Might you be managing sadly? Bitterly? Resentfully? What about regretfully or half-heartedly? There are so many possible ways to manage.

Here's my suggestion: if you're not managing gracefully or you're nowhere near that neighborhood, consider firing the manager. When sports franchises or big businesses are suffering, it is not uncommon to fire the manager and bring in a new manager with a completely different style of management. If you're managing poorly, you may need to replace yourself with a new you who manages gracefully, thus increasing the likelihood of your being happier.

As I consider what it means to manage gracefully, here are some principles to keep in mind:

1) Try to take things less personally. It's not just you who's struggling. Life is hard and is full of

challenges. Everyone is dealing with demons and fighting some kind of battle.

2) Remember the proverbial, "This too shall pass."

3) Treat yourself and others with compassion and kindness.

4) Continue to value life and feel gratitude, even if circumstances are difficult.

You've heard of anger management and stress management. Adhering to the four principles outlined above is grace management. Life will never be "just a bowl of cherries." There will always be pits, a few rotten cherries, and the like. This is not Shangri-La, but you can practice managing gracefully right here and right now.

NAUSEA

It was early afternoon on a beautiful June day when I suddenly felt sick to my stomach. The nausea engulfed me. It felt like I was a stone's throw away from vomiting. I had no idea why but briefly entertained the idea that I might have a virus. I didn't. The nausea persisted. It preoccupied me. No matter where I went or what I was doing, it was omnipresent. It would come in waves and some were worse than others. The nausea lasted all day. And the next. And the day after that. I lightened my work schedule and did very little socially. I figured that I'd wait it out, thinking each day would be the last day I'd feel so queasy. It didn't cease. After three full weeks of unwavering nausea, the doctor examined me, did labwork, and sent me for CAT scans, a colonoscopy, and an endoscopy.

All the test results were fine. There was no physiological explanation for my nausea. Although I greatly respect my doctor's opinion, when he suggested that it might have been a lingering virus, I intuitively knew that was not it. After all, I am a pretty decent psychologist, and I know the power of psychological issues in producing a vast array of physical symptoms. I had recently successfully treated a woman who practically went blind because of psychological factors—literally not wanting to see things that were happening in her life.

I decided to try to understand my nausea from a psychological perspective. I remembered that one of Jean Paul Sartre's books was titled *Nausea* and that I read it decades ago. Sure enough, I was able to find the 1969 copy of it in a box of old books. It was about a diary kept by a French writer named Antoine Roquentin. He wrote, "...the nausea seized me," and "I wanted to vomit. And since that time, the nausea has not left me; it holds me." The book chronicled his philosophical and psychological struggles to come to terms with his existence. The book provided Sartre with a vehicle to express the basic tenets of existentialism, which deal with the so-called "absurdity" of life and what is termed "nothingness." Roquentin states:

> The truth stares me in the face; this man
> is going to die soon. He surely knows; he
> need only look in the glass; each day he
> looks a little more like the corpse he will
> become.

Aha! The light bulb went on. The following events preceded my nausea:

(1) Physical inactivity. I had run regularly for the past 40 years or so. But a stress fracture of the heel and a cracked rib from falling

off my mountain bike propelled me into a somewhat sedentary existence that I was not used to. I could no longer run, hike, or bike, and I couldn't even walk for exercise. On top of that, insult was added to injury when the MRI of my heel cited "degenerative" changes.

(2) A friend of mine who had just celebrated his 60th birthday took ill and died shortly thereafter.

(3) Shortly after awakening one morning, I looked in the mirror and saw my mother's face instead of my own. She was in her 90s when she died some years ago, but my face morphed into hers as I viewed myself in the glass. Remember Roquentin's statement noted earlier in this story: each day he looks a little more like the corpse he will become.

I'm guessing my nausea reflected an existential crisis of sorts. I'm used to being healthy and very active. Being thrust into a sedentary position and hearing the word "degenerative" used in connection with my health didn't sit well with me. I'm not fond of thinking of my own death. I guess when I'm running, biking, and hiking, it provides the illusion of immortality, which I don't mind buying into. When my friend died, it brought my mortality to the forefront. You can run, but you can't hide. Make that: I couldn't run (literally) and I couldn't hide. Unable to do my usual recreational activities, I began to feel less well and closer to death. Having pain with each step, I remember having the thought, "Is this what it's like to be old?"

Shortly thereafter is when I looked in the mirror and my face looked old and drawn and became the face of my mother. I guess that the right combination of events occurring in a short period of time produced symptoms in me — psychogenic nausea with no physiological basis. So, I did what I always do: I practiced what I preached. I decided again that just because we die, it doesn't make life meaningless or absurd. I never took the Compazine or the Nexium that were prescribed for the nausea. Instead, I took hefty doses of my own prescriptions. I focused on what I could do and did whatever I was capable of doing in a wholehearted way. I reminded myself daily to be patient and to be grateful. I aligned myself with hope and humor rather than with hopelessness and despair. I focused on thinking reasonably. I told myself that most 64-year-olds have degenerative changes and that the likelihood of my being nauseous the rest of my life was unlikely. I began to write more and decided that I might have many years left and that I didn't want to sit around preoccupied with thinking about my own death. Life is not absurd if I continue to create meaning through my choices and a leap of faith.

It took about three and a half weeks. I had figured out what the nausea was about and what created it. I confronted it head on, accepted the anxiety, and found ways to resolve it. The nausea went away. My intuition was correct. Indeed, it was psychological — unless it was simply a virus.

> I finally understand what life is about;
> It is about losing everything....
> So every morning we must celebrate what we have.
> –Isabelle Allende

THE OLD WOMAN OF THE SEALS

There is an ancient Eskimo tale that Joseph Campbell recounts in his epic work *Primitive Mythology*. The old woman of the seals sits in her dwelling. It is here that she casts her spells or sends her blessings, this being the determinant of whether she sends forth or withholds the animals that feed the Eskimo people — fish, seals, walruses, and whales. One day, filthy parasites attach themselves to her long hair and head. Angry, ill, and in pain, the old woman neglects her usual rituals. The food supply of animals to the people dwindles. The village elders decide that a highly competent shaman undertake the very dangerous journey to the dwelling of the old woman of the seals so as to relieve her of her pain.

The way is fraught with many obstacles and difficulties. The shaman encounters an abyss that he must cross by negotiating a wheel that is slippery as ice and always turning. He must traverse a gigantic boiling kettle that is full of dangerous seals, after which he arrives at the old woman's dwelling. It is guarded by terrible beasts, ravenous dogs, and biting seals. When he finally enters the house itself, he must cross an abyss by means of a bridge as narrow as the edge of a knife. He does so and relieves her of her parasites, pain, and wrath. The food supply is restored and the shaman returns to the village. The old woman, the shaman, the village elders and the Eskimo people are all happier, resulting from the shaman's persistence and resiliency. He faced perils, negotiated obstacles, and accepted the challenges.

You have a shaman in you. That shaman part of your self may be dormant. Maybe it has never been awakened, but it is there, like a sleeping giant. You have untapped strength and unrealized courage. You can do very difficult things.

The shaman who faced all those dangers in dealing with the old woman of the seals was not larger than life. He probably got discouraged and felt like giving up at times, but he didn't. A Norwegian proverb has it that heroism is "hanging on one minute longer." Norman Vincent Peale said, "It's always too early to quit." You may be discouraged. You may not feel strong enough or courageous enough to face difficult challenges. Don't sell yourself short. Get in touch with the shaman part of you. Heal the old woman of the seals. The challenge in and of itself is worthwhile.

OVER THE WALL

Peter Conradi, Professor Emeritus at Kingston University in London, tells a very moving story that is both heartbreaking and heartwarming. It is hard not to be deeply touched by this story that he heard while living in Poland:

> Around 1943, Jews were being rounded up and herded into cattle trucks going to the gas chambers of Treblinka. They knew that death was imminent. The square was filled with horrified, malnourished mothers and their children. They passed their babies over their heads from one pair of upraised hands to another until the babies got close to a high wall that contained them. The babies were then thrown over the wall, where caring Catholic Polish

> women waited. These Catholic women caught the Jewish babies and brought them up as Gentiles.

Can you imagine what it must have been like for the women to throw their babies over the wall? In their terror, they found the courage and wherewithal to act boldly and decisively. How many conflicting feelings must they have had simultaneously? In the most horrible of times, they were able to make a commitment that saved their babies' lives. And the Catholic Polish women's courage, compassion, and commitment were also necessary to save those lives. Humanity and love transcended the labels of Jew and Catholic.

Tal Ben-Shaher, who teaches a course on happiness at Harvard, poses the following:

> Imagine your life as a journey. You are walking, knapsack on your back, making good progress, until suddenly, you reach a brick wall that stands in the way of reaching your destination. What do you do? Do you turn around and avoid the challenge posed by the barrier? Or, do you take the opposite approach and throw your knapsack over the wall, thus committing yourself to finding ways of getting through, around, or over the wall?

The importance of commitment cannot be overstated. If you believe you can get over the wall and make a commitment to doing so, you greatly increase your chances of it happening. If you've ever had the feeling that you can move mountains, so to speak, or that the gods were smiling upon you, it most likely stemmed from the decisiveness of bold action. Is there a situation in your life now that is frustrating or confusing? Have you waffled with regard to what to do? Is it diminishing your happiness? Make a decision. Committing yourself wholeheartedly to that decision will turn it into the right decision for you. Go ahead. Throw your knapsack over the wall.

You don't stop dancing because of growing old.
You grow old when you stop dancing.

IX.
AGING
&
DEATH

The idea is to die young as late as possible.
–Ashley Montagu

GRIN AND BEAR IT

I was enjoying my morning run as I rounded the bend of a rural mountain road. In an instant, I was face to face with a very large bear (who gets a little bigger each time I tell the story). Screeching to a halt, I immediately registered that this was a brown bear. I was pretty sure that brown bears were vegetarians, but then I thought, "What if he's off his diet?"

To say I was frightened would be an understatement. As our eyes met, I remembered an article that stated bears could climb better and run faster than humans. That article advised that if you encounter a bear, you should lie down and play dead. I thought, "Yeah, right. What were they thinking?" For a split second, I must have hallucinated, as it looked to me as if the bear were wearing Reeboks. He wasn't.

The bear and I were motionless, about 10 yards apart, staring at each other. My life did not flash in front of me. I considered that a good sign. I slowly backed up, never losing eye contact with the bear. One step at a time, backing up until I was around the bend and the bear was out of sight. Then I turned and ran as fast as I could. I may have run faster than I ever had before.

Several times, I looked over my left shoulder as I ran. I remembered the advice given to Carlos Castaneda by the wise Yaqui Indian Sorcerer Don Juan. He told him that if he looks over his left shoulder, he will see his death stalking him, ready to tap him on the shoulder at any time. This was not meant to depress Carlos, but rather to get him to understand that there isn't a moment to lose, and that he needs to roll up his sleeves, put things in perspective, and make choices.

I frequently think of that gigantic (it just grew a little more) brown bear staring at me. But more often than that, I think of what Don Juan told Carlos. I look over my left shoulder and use my death stalking me as if he were a wise sage. I don't ruminate. And, I don't waffle back and forth. I decide. I choose. I act. And, in retrospect, I'm glad I decided not to lie down and play dead when I came face to face with that humongous bear.

THE BAGEL STORE

I'm in a bagel store. The guy in front of me is in a conversation with the guy who's filling his order. They both appear to be in their early twenties. As the customer waits for his bagel with bacon, eggs, and cheese, they discuss the pros and cons of the Barry Bonds steroid case. It's difficult not to listen to their conversation. They are both talking in louder-than-normal conversational tones:

> Customer: Would you take steroids to make twenty million a year even if you knew they'd kill you by fifty?
>
> Counter Guy: Of course!
>
> Customer: Damn right!

It didn't seem to be a difficult decision for either of them. Neither required more than an instant to agree on the answer. I guess it was a no-brainer for them. Ah, the naïvete of youth.

Fifty years old must have sounded like an eternity away. If they only knew ....

Inside every 50-year-old is a 20-year-old saying, "What happened?"

THINKING ABOUT THAT BAGEL STORE

Billy and I went to college together. We were fraternity brothers. Neither one of us was even in the neighborhood of maturity. We had a great time—played sports, partied, double dated, drank more than our fair share, and occasionally studied. Life was good. Our late teens and early 20s were filled with adventure. It wasn't exactly sex, drugs, and rock and roll. It was more like sex, beer, basketball, and rock and roll. This was the early 1960s. We were immortal.

Fast forward 45 years. Billy and I are talking on the phone. When we interact, we're still capable of being quite immature, but we have grown up. During the hour on the phone, we discuss different topics than in the old days. Not only are we no longer immortal, our mortality is around the corner. We still talk sports and music, but there are new topics that take up the bulk of this phone conversation—grandchildren, Viagra, health issues,

Medicare, and what age to begin taking Social Security are all discussed in detail. Yes, everything changes, but some things stay the same—like our friendship. The lyrics are different, but the melody is the same.

Our youth is behind us. We're not as strong as we once were. We look older. We can't run as fast or jump as high. But there is still so much to do. There are still adventures. There is more peace of mind. And, we still double date.

I'm reminded of Tennyson's *Ulysses*. Odysseus, after a grueling war and many hair-raising and conflictual experiences, finally arrives home to reunite with his faithful Penelope. After much reflection, Odysseus says:

> Though much is taken, much abides;
> and though we are not now the strength
> which in old days moved earth and heaven;
> that which we are we are.

THE END OF THE WORLD

Sylvia Boorstein writes of her father's seven-year struggle with multiple myeloma, an incurable cancer:

> One day, when his illness was quite advanced, his spirits seemed particularly flagging. The day loomed long before us, and I said, "Let's go to a movie." He looked at me, seemingly incredulous, and said, "You know, I'm *dying*!" I said, "Yes, I know, but not today." We saw *Raiders of the Lost Ark*. We both loved it. We had dinner at the Pacific Café, his favorite restaurant.
>
> and ...

When my father was dying, I remained at his bedside for his final days. The last few days of his life he was primarily in a coma from which he would rouse from time to time. We knew he was dying, and we were making him as comfortable as we could, waiting for his last breath. Every once in a while he would seem to breathe his last: his body would shake and he'd have the kind of apnea that people do when they are dying. I would hold his hand and say my prepared speech: "Go to the light" and "Now is your chance to get out of this body." I'm pleased that I did that; those are all the right things to say when someone is dying. ("You've done a good job in this lifetime." "Everybody loved you." "It's time to move on." "You don't need this old body anymore.") Each time he would struggle with his last breath, I would give him the speech again. Then he would relax and fall asleep, and I would go back to waiting. Very near the end, he began a siege of apnea, and I leaped to my feet, beginning my talk about "Go to the light." He opened his eyes, and he looked at me and said quite clearly, "You know, it's not that big of a deal."

But, of course, we do think and feel that death is that big of a deal. As I write this in 2009, there are many reports, television shows, and abundant websites devoted to Nostradamus and the forthcoming end of the world on December 21, 2012. Supposedly, the ancient Mayan calendar, the medieval predictions of Merlin, and the Chinese oracle of the I Ching all point to that date as being the end of civilization as we know it. When a 16th century "lost" book by Nostradamus was discovered at the National Library in Rome by journalist Enza Massa, the media and cultists and doomsday forecasters from all corners of the globe were off and running.

In case you're not familiar with him, Nostradamus was a French apothecary who evolved into a mystical seer and published prophecies that were vague and subject to varied interpretations. His elusive style in which he employed metaphorical and cryptic language may have been necessary so as to avoid persecution based on his beliefs. However, that same style has insured his immortality as people essentially interpret his writings as they wish, kind of the way a person looks at a Rorschach ink blot and tells you what she sees.

I wouldn't advise you to give a lot of credence to December 21, 2012, being the end of the world. On December 20, it's probably not a good idea to tell off your boss, admit to your affair, go to confession, or eat ice cream, chocolate, and french fries the whole day. The predicted end of the world has come and gone many times before. If you're going to think seriously about your demise, it will not be in your best interest if you become immobilized or consumed with fear.

In the cult classic, *The Hitchhiker's Guide to the Galaxy*, it was on a Thursday when the feeling was prevalent that the earth was about to be destroyed:

Barman:	Did you say the world is coming to an end? Shouldn't we all lie on the floor or put paper bags over our heads?
Ford:	If you like.
Barman:	Will it help?
Ford:	Not at all.

We all know that we are finite, mortal beings. We all know about death, but please make sure that you're living your life well and courageously. Don't sit around waiting to die with a paper bag over your head.

Millions long for immortality
who do not know what to do with
themselves on a rainy Sunday afternoon.
–Susan Ertz

FACE TO FACE

Many years ago, my mother and I were being stalked by a man wearing dark clothing. Although we couldn't get a good look at him, he had a powerful presence and was definitely after us. In the blackness of an eerie night, we fled to escape from him. We ran from one place to another, growing wearier with each new effort to find safety. We hid again and again, but when we felt the terror of his getting closer, we'd run to find another hiding spot.

We settled into an old apartment building and hid under a stairway. Our breathing was labored and our hearts were pounding. My elderly mother said, "I'm exhausted. I can't run anymore." I answered, "You have to. He's getting closer." That's when we heard the door of the apartment building creak open. We knew it was him. The only sound was of his footsteps getting closer and closer to us. We feared for our lives. From my position under the stairwell, I could see his feet. He knew we were there.

I came out from under the stairwell. It was dark and I still couldn't see him clearly. Much of his face was covered, but his eyes met mine. We stood face to face about two feet apart from each other. I looked directly in his eyes. Neither of us broke eye contact. Neither of us blinked. He extended his right arm and he was holding a gun. He put the barrel of the gun against my forehead. I was no longer afraid. He pulled the trigger and shot me in the head. He fired six shots altogether as I continued to look him in the eye. Nothing happened. He turned and left.

We were okay. My mother and I left the old building and began walking down the middle of the street. Music began playing. All along the route, people were coming out of hiding and walking with us. It seemed a bit like the end of a Broadway show, where all the characters gathered for the musical finale. We were alive and happy. That was the end of my dream.

I related it to a colleague who was psychoanalytically oriented, and he said that it was a classic Oedipal Complex resolution dream. His interpretation left me flat. When tears came to his eyes as he was interpreting my dream, I began to believe that his interpretation had more to do with him than with me. To me, it seemed like the dream was about death stalking me. After running away repeatedly, I decided to face up to the whole predicament.

> ... the acceptance of human destiny is the way to put one's feet on solid ground. We then are not the ready prey of hobgoblins — we are no longer fighting battles against figments of our imagination; no boogeyman is lurking in the closet. We are freed from the hundred and one imagi-

nary bonds; we are loosed from the need
to beg others to take care of us. Having
confronted the worst, we are released to
open up to the possibilities of life.

> –Rollo May

It were as if I was saying to death, "Okay. Here I am. Give it your best shot." And death gave it his best six shots. There was the realization that there was nothing to run from. Death is an inescapable part of life, and being conscious of that and facing it with both eyes wide open leads to the Broadway show finale.

I'm reminded of a Steely Dan song called "Bad Sneakers":

> Do you take me for a fool?
> Do you think that I don't see?
> That ditch out in the valley
> That they're digging just for me?

Facing your death is really the equivalent of fully embracing life and rolling up your sleeves to produce joy and purpose.

> We are here to laugh at the odds
> and live our lives so well
> that Death will tremble to take us.
> –Charles Bukowski

IF I ONLY KNEW THEN
WHAT I KNOW NOW!

When God became upset with Adam and Eve, he decided to take happiness away from them. An advisor suggested he put happiness far, far away, but God knew people would travel to the ends of the earth looking for it. Another advisor suggested putting it at the bottom of the ocean, but God knew that people would dive to the ocean bed in search of it. A third advisor suggested putting happiness on the highest of mountains. But God knew that they would scale any mountain peak. Aha, the answer came to him in a flash. God said, "I've got it. I'll put happiness inside them. They'll never think to look for it there!"

In the book *Happier*, the author asks you to imagine that you are one hundred and ten years old with all of your faculties. You have acquired a lifetime of experience and wisdom. A time machine is invented that will transport you back in time. You will have fifteen minutes to spend with your younger self. You'll have the opportunity to talk with and give advice to the younger you. What will you say?

My brother Bruce was given only months to live. When he was given that death sentence, he had an epiphany with respect to how he should live his life. Ben-Shahar points out that this often happens with terminally ill patients. Isn't it fascinating that these are the same people with the same knowledge of life, the same histories as before, and the same intellects and emotional dispositions that they had prior to receiving the news of their terminal illnesses? They now know what their priorities should be, what matters most, what is trivial in the overall scheme of things, and what isn't. And all of this occurred without sitting at the feet of gurus, prophets, or sages, without taking courses, without using mind altering drugs, and without reading *The Happiness Solution*.

This goes to show that they already had within them the answers to how to live life and be happy. The answers were there, but they never looked seriously for them, never giving them the attention they should have – that is until they got the diagnosis of being terminally ill. You know how to live your life. You have the answers and the wisdom. Don't wait until time machines are invented in order to share your wisdom with yourself. Don't wait until you're terminally ill. As Jung said, "Life is like a terminal illness since it is the condition of which the prognosis is death." What are you waiting for?

THE LAST LECTURE

If you were a college professor and were asked to give one last lecture before you died, what would you say? Dr. Randy Pausch, a computer science professor at Carnegie Mellon University, was recently put in that position. Dr. Pausch was a 46-year-old married father of three young children. He had 10 tumors in his liver and was dying of cancer. His doctors had given him a prognosis of decent health for a few months before deteriorating health and impending death would arrive. Here's part of his now-infamous lecture:

> Apologize when you screw up and focus on other people, not on yourself. And I thought, how do I possibly make a concrete example of that? [Speaking to stage hand] Do we have a concrete example of focusing on somebody else over there?

Could we bring it out? [Speaking to audience] See, yesterday was my wife's birthday. If there was ever a time I might be entitled to have the focus on me, it might be the last lecture. But no, I feel very badly that my wife didn't really get a proper birthday, and I thought it would be very nice if 500 people— [An oversized birthday cake is wheeled onto the stage and all sing happy birthday to his wife, Jai.]

This is deathbed-type wisdom. The man was rapidly dying and was still not preoccupied with himself. He was still being kind, loving, and generous. He said, "I mean, I don't know how to not have fun. I'm dying and I'm having fun. And I'm going to keep having fun every day I have left, because there's no other way to play it."

Other parts of his last lecture focused on the following themes:

–Complain less
–Work hard at being good at something
–Find the best in everybody
–Show gratitude
–Be honest
–Be patient with others
–If your kids want to paint their bedrooms, let them
–Lead your life the right way
–Be prepared

After saying that we can't change the cards we are dealt—just how we play the hand—Dr. Pausch apologized to the overflow crowd. "If I don't seem as depressed or morose as I should be, sorry to disappoint you."

It reminds me of a story I read in a book called *Graceful Exits: How Great Beings Die*:

> When Zen Master Tung-shan felt it was time for him to go, he had his head shaved, took a bath, put on his robe, rang the bell to bid farewell to the community, and sat up till he breathed no more. To all appearances, he had died. Thereupon the whole community burst out crying grievously as little children do at the death of their mother. Suddenly the master opened his eyes and said to the weeping monks, "We monks are supposed to be detached from all things transitory. In this consists true spiritual life. To live is to work, to die is to rest. What is the use of groaning and moaning?" He then ordered a "stupidity-purifying" meal for the whole community. After the meal he said to them, "Please make no fuss over me! Be calm as befits a family of monks! Generally speaking, when anyone is at the point of going, he has no use for noise and commotion." Thereupon he returned to the Abbot's room, where he sat in meditation until he passed away.

The book was written by Sushila Blackman. She was a student of the Hindu Master Swami Muktananda. She was in India at his ashram when he died. Months before she finished *Graceful Exits*, she was diagnosed with advanced lung cancer. She died peacefully six weeks after finishing the book. She wrote, "In the Zen tradition, to die is nothing special," and "…to the Zen Buddhist, the solution to life's enigma is to be found within one's own mind." Zen has a lot to do with simplicity and "suchness," which extend to one's dying moments.

> Annihilation has no terrors for me, because I have already tried it before I was born—a hundred million years…. There was a peace, a serenity, an absence of all sense of responsibility, an absence of worry, an absence of care, grief, perplexity; and the presence of a deep content and unbroken satisfaction in that hundred million years of holiday, which I look back upon with a tender longing and with a grateful desire to resume, when the opportunity comes.
>
> –Mark Twain

I am not trying to romanticize death. Being conscious of and grappling with the facts that we and everyone we love will die is the most difficult thing we have to come to terms with. I don't know what happens after we die, but I do know how important it is to live fully and feel good about the life you're living for as long as you can. Dr. Pausch gave a last lecture that I'll never forget. Fun, gratitude, grace, acceptance, kindness, compassion, vitality, humor, love, freedom, faith. It was all there.

221

One night after a dharma talk, I asked Suzuki Roshi a question about life and death.
The answer he gave made my fear of
death, for that moment, pop like a bubble.

He looked at me and said, "You will always exist in the universe in some form."
−from *Zen Is Right Here*
(edited by David Chadwick)

WOULD YOU LIKE BOTOX WITH THAT?

85, 86, 87, 88, 89, 90. I'm not counting. Those are the ages of some of my psychology patients. For some of them, I make house calls. It's been estimated that by the year 2030, there will be well over 70 million people in the United States who will be 65 or older. The road to growing old can be fraught with perils, especially in our society that values and is obsessed with youth.

In our frantic efforts to not see signs of aging when we look in the mirror, we search for the ever-elusive fountain of youth. Botox, facials, herbal therapies, anti-aging cosmetics, and plastic surgery have us spending many billions of dollars. As it turns out, there is no fountain of youth. Nobody gets out of here alive. This is not Greek mythology. Alas, we are all mortals. With Botox parties replacing Tupperware parties, the anti-aging illusion is perpetuated, but it is all illusion. We can only fool ourselves for so long.

The antidote to aging and dying is to live as well as you can. Being less concerned with aging and more concerned with creating a life you feel good about is in the interest of happiness. John Steinbeck wrote, "And in my own life I am not willing to trade quality for quantity." He also stated, "I see too many men delay their exits with a sickly, slow reluctance to leave the stage. It's bad theatre as well as bad living."

Of course, we all hope for long and happy disability-free lives. But we never know exactly what we're going to get. We need to make our peace with aging. It's not such a bad thing. We need to stop devaluing the aged and come to terms with growing older. Hopefully, we'll all get a turn to be old. The closest we'll get to a fountain of youth will be the result of living our lives with curiosity, courage, open-mindedness, enthusiasm, kindness, optimism, humor, love, and gratitude.

The noted psychologist Erik Erikson theorizes that life goes through a series of eight stages of development, with each stage having a psychosocial crisis. In each stage, the person either successfully resolves or fails to resolve the crisis. The final stage in life occurs in the so-called senior years. The crisis dealt with in the final stages of life has to do with whether you will die with integrity or despair.

As you reflect back on your life and review it, you will reach a sense as to whether your life was a success or a failure. If you feel very disappointed in your life and feel that you have wasted it and have many regrets, you will be left despairing. If you feel a general sense of having done your best and having lived well, you will have achieved integrity, thus attaining wisdom, even as death approaches.

Happiness is not about not aging and not dying. It's about finding meaning and taking pride in your life. You know how you read a movie review and the reviewer gives it no stars to four stars? Review and rate your life. If it's anything under three stars, start to rewrite the story. Rewrite it vigorously. You still have some time to turn it into a three or four-star life. This way, you'll be happier and that final stage of your life will find you with integrity rather than despair.

> Life is not a journey to the grave with the intention of arriving safely in a pretty, well-preserved body ... but rather to skid in broadside, thoroughly used up, totally worn out, and loudly proclaiming ... WOW! WHAT A RIDE!
>
> –Anonymous

Nobody cares if you can't dance well.
Just get up and dance. Great dancers are
not great because of their technique;
they are great because of their passion.
–Martha Graham

X.
SHOWING UP FOR
YOUR OWN LIFE

Work like you don't need the money,
love like you've never been hurt,
and dance like no one is watching.
–Satchel Paige

GO FOR IT

It was spring 1966. I was walking across campus when I spotted a girl I had never seen before. I was a senior, so I guessed that she had to be a freshman. It was a small campus and I knew most of the kids who went there. I was immediately attracted to this new girl and asked a friend I was walking with if he knew who she was. He told me her name and I looked it up in the campus phonebook. I called her.

My first words to her were, "You don't know me, but...." She didn't hang up on me, but she wasn't particularly receptive either. She asked me a bunch of questions related to her trying to figure out who I was: where I sat in the student union, what fraternity I was in, who I hung around with, and so on. In her mind, she narrowed it down to my being one of the two people she could picture. She knew she was on the phone with either me or my friend Billy. Since she knew neither of us by name, when I told her my name was Alan, it didn't help her distinguish between us. Billy, by the way, was this hot-looking athletic guy, so she continued her phone conversation with me.

I asked her if she wanted to go out that night. She told me that she had a date at eight o'clock. I told her I'd stop by at seven just to introduce myself and that she could still go on her date. She said no way. I persevered politely. She wavered. I sensed it: I had a feeling she could be the one. I continued my polite perseverance. She acquiesced. I later found out that the only reason she agreed to meet me was that she thought she was speaking to Billy.

At seven o'clock that night, I picked her up outside her apartment and we went for a ride. It was probably more of love at first sight for me than it was for her, but we did hit it off right off the bat. I brought her home about a half hour late for her date. I called her the next day and we began going out. Three and a half years later, Nan and I were married. My life was forever changed for the better because I decided to take action. I had decided to go for it and call a 17-year-old girl who didn't even know my name.

Remember Billy, the guy who Nan really wanted to meet? At that time, he was dating Sherry. My roommate, Tony, saw her and asked me if I knew who she was. I told him that I knew her, but that she and Billy were an item. He said to me, "I'm going to marry her!" Being that he didn't even know her and being that she was with Billy, it was hard to imagine that happening. Anyhow, I introduced Tony to Sherry. Years later, I was best man at their wedding.

Billy fell in love with Joyce, and they married. Over 40 years since all of this began unfolding, Tony and Sherry, Billy and Joyce, and Nan and I still get together and share our lives. Everyone remembers the events of those days a little differently, but we can laugh at all of our versions of the truth.

I don't think you find happiness by sitting on the fence. Don't be tentative when it comes to decision making that has to do with following your heart. Go for it. Go for it tenaciously. Give it your all. I went for it in the spring of 1966. I'm happy I did.

> If my doctor told me I had only six minutes to live,
> I wouldn't brood. I'd type a little faster.
> –Isaac Asimov

STILL BAKING AFTER
ALL THESE YEARS

Inchoate \in-KOH-it\ means in an early stage or imperfectly formed or formulated. It is from the Latin incohare, which means to begin. I continually remind people that they are not finished products. It's as if they are still baking. Indeed, you are a work in progress. As long as you're alive, you're still baking. Once you believe you're done, you're done — figuratively, and perhaps, literally.

Life is all about change. Learning, failing, trying, experimenting, relearning. Adapting, erring, evolving, waiting, growing, maturing, and choosing. I've worked with people who think they're done baking. Generally speaking, they're unhappy and feel like there's nothing to look forward to. They lack vision, imagination, optimism, and faith. They are walking and talking death-like equivalents. I need to convince them to get back in the oven. They think they're fully baked, but I'm certain they're half-baked (pun intended).

Jack was 75 years old when he came in for therapy. His wife had died a couple of years back. His son and daughter were married and lived about 45 minutes away. He was retired, had an old house, an old car, and was depressed. As far as he was concerned, for all intents and purposes, his life was over. In essence, he was waiting to die. He didn't want to do anything, felt overwhelmed by his old house, and didn't travel much because of his old car. Jack needed to get back in the oven.

Over the next year, Jack agreed begrudgingly to continue baking. He was able to get rid of his old car and lease a new one. This enabled him to travel to see his children and grandchildren without fearing the car would break down. He was able to sell his house and move to an apartment that was more manageable for him. He reluctantly agreed to join organizations and volunteer two days a week at a local hospital. He met new people, socialized more, and joined a gym where he worked out four days a week. At the gym, he also took yoga classes. He met a woman he liked very much and they began to see each other regularly. They traveled. He was no longer waiting to die.

Jack may have been a senior citizen when I met him, but I knew he was an inchoate human being who was still a work in progress. Aren't we all? Excuse me. Time to get back in the oven for a bit.

DON'T JUST SIT THERE, DO SOMETHING

Put up or shut up. Put your money where your mouth is. Don't just talk the talk; walk the walk. Yes, you've heard all the platitudes about the importance of taking action. Have the courage of your convictions. Too many people are having near-life experiences. If you believe in something strongly, take a stand. Help out. Go out of your way. Do something charitable. Roll up your sleeves. Immerse yourself in it. It's not enough to think about it. Do it. Get started now.

Be ignited, or be gone.
–Mary Oliver

TRUST ME ON THIS ONE

Many years ago, I was running an inpatient therapy group at a state psychiatric facility. It was my first day there. After introducing myself, I asked the seven patients to tell me their names, prefacing it by saying that it might take me some time to remember all their names. As it turned out, it wasn't going to be that hard. The first young man simply said, "I'm Jesus Christ." When another man told me that he was Jesus Christ, I thought, "This is going to be interesting." I didn't blink an eye when the last gentleman to introduce himself said, "My name is Jesus Christ."

Thinking back to an old TV game show called "To Tell the Truth," I almost shouted, "Will the real Jesus Christ please stand up." I didn't. I was able to control myself, thankfully. Three Jesuses in the same group — more validation that life is fascinating. With paranoid schizophrenia, the Jesus delusion is not a rare occurrence. It naturally encompasses both delusions of grandeur and delusions of persecution. It may seem kind of crazy, but psychologically and spiritually speaking, it's a beautifully crafted and meaningful delusion. Years ago, I wrote a scholarly treatise on the subject that was published and is referenced at the back of this book.

Years later, I ran a walk-in group each morning at a community mental health center. I'd put up a coffee pot and see if anyone showed up. Most of the people who did were psychotic, usually schizophrenic. We'd talk about whatever they wanted to. One of my regulars was a guy named Terry who also believed he was Jesus Christ. We spoke regularly about the joys and burdens of being Jesus. He felt he was doing a world of good.

One of the points to be made here is that everyone wants to matter. You and me too. It's not necessary to be famous or to be Jesus in order to matter. Of course you matter. Do you love someone? Does someone love you? Have you ever been kind or compassionate or generous of spirit? Everything you do matters. Becoming schizophrenic largely stems from a fundamental mistrust of one's environment and one's self. Trust who you are and know that you matter.

Oriah Mountain Dreamer has written a beautiful prose poem titled "The Invitation":

It doesn't interest me what you do for a living.
I want to know what you ache for,
and if you dare to dream
of meeting your heart's longing.

It doesn't interest me how old you are.
I want to know if you will risk

looking like a fool for love,
for your dream,
for the adventure of being alive.

It doesn't interest me what planets
are squaring your moon.
I want to know if you have touched
the center of your own sorrow,
if you have been opened by life's betrayals
or have become shriveled and closed
from fear of further pain.

I want to know if you can sit with pain,
mine or your own,
without moving to hide it or fade it,
or fix it.

I want to know if you can be with joy,
mine or your own,
if you can dance with wildness
and let the ecstasy fill you
to the tips of your fingers and toes
without cautioning us to be careful,
be realistic,
to remember the limitations of being human.

It doesn't interest me if the story
you are telling me is true.
I want to know if you can disappoint
another to be true to yourself;
if you can bear the accusation of betrayal

and not betray your own soul;
if you can be faithless
and therefore trustworthy.

I want to know if you can see beauty
even when it is not pretty,
every day,
and if you can source your own life
from its presence.

I want to know if you can live with failure,
yours and mine,
and still stand on the edge of the lake
and shout to the silver of the full moon,
"Yes!"

It doesn't interest me to know where you live
or how much money you have.
I want to know if you can get up,
after the night of grief and despair,
weary and bruised to the bone,
and do what needs to be done
to feed the children.

It doesn't interest me who you know
or how you came to be here.
I want to know if you will stand
in the center of the fire with me
and not shrink back.

It doesn't interest me where or what
or with whom you have studied.
I want to know what sustains you,
from the inside,
when all else falls away.

I want to know if you can
be alone with yourself
and if you truly like the company
you keep in the empty moments.

ALL ALONE

I'm all alone driving to Cape Cod on a brisk, late-fall morning. The sky is as blue as a sky can be. There are enormous, puffy cotton cumulus clouds that appear as if they are being viewed through 3D glasses. Sipping on a cup of hot chocolate and listening to music with the volume turned up, I feel great. Now, I'm singing at the top of my lungs, doing a duet with Tracy Chapman:

> Baby can I hold you tonight?
> Baby if I said the right thing,
> At the right time,
> Would you be mine?

This scene goes on for quite a while as I engage in mind-bending duets with Tom Waits, Dylan, The Crash Test Dummies, Dire Straits, and various other collaborators. Life is good.

It strikes me that some of the most enjoyable or meaningful

times for me occur when I'm alone. I like that fact. It means that I get along with myself very well. I'm a good friend to me. It's not that I don't have wonderful times with others, but alone times can also be special. Praying is usually a solitary activity that is very special for me. Meditation is another thing I generally do by myself. Both prayer and meditation have had an immeasurable impact on my life.

Most days, I run by myself and have had an incredible range of unforgettable emotions and experiences while running. At times, I hike by myself and also do photo shoots that have been enormously gratifying. And, of course, when I'm alone is the time that I write my books on haiku, Zen, wabi-sabi, and removing obstacles to happiness.

I hope you also enjoy your time alone. Are you capable of entertaining yourself? Are you a good friend to you—patient, tolerant, compassionate, caring, and encouraging? I hope you have solitary activities or pursuits that you enjoy or are deeply committed to. If not, it is certainly worth the effort to find whatever it takes for you to love to be with yourself.

> Is not life a hundred times too
> short for us to bore ourselves?
> –Friedrich Nietzsche

ACCEPTANCE

Most psychotherapists will tell you that unhappiness is directly related to a person's insistence that his or her world should be different than it is. Putting it another way, the gap between how you see what's happening in your life and what you wish were happening is directly related to your well-being or lack of it. The bigger the gap, the more frustration, disappointment, depression, resentment, blame, and anger.

I often work with patients to help them narrow that gap. Sometimes, obsessing over what they think is wrong with their lives only tends to magnify it. I often remind them that there is a big difference between a tragedy and a disappointment — between a disaster and things not working out perfectly. We need to understand that life will never be exactly as we would like it to be. And we need to do more than simply pay lip service to this. We have to accept it — and live that acceptance.

Don't confuse acceptance with resignation, selling out, not

trying to better yourself or your life, or with allowing others to take advantage of you—that's not what I'm suggesting. The quality of our lives depends on how we look at things. We can learn to accept life even if it's not a script we would be writing. The very fact of acceptance often changes our emotional state for the better. As soon as we open ourselves to accepting a difficult situation, it becomes less difficult. Our suffering is often related to our clinging to the idea that the situation needs to be different than it is in order to feel better about it. Acceptance has to do with taking what life offers and making room for all your feelings. In *The Happiness Trap*, Russ Harris addresses this:

> Acceptance doesn't mean you have to like your uncomfortable thoughts and feelings; it just means you stop struggling with them. When you stop wasting your energy on trying to change, avoid, or get rid of them, you can put that energy into something more useful instead.

In her book *Everyday Zen*, Zen Master Charlotte Joko Beck talks about cultivating the ability to stand back from your feelings and your problems and become "A Bigger Container." By doing this, you are able to accommodate more of life so you're much less likely to feel overwhelmed and much more likely to have peace of mind. As you're able to accept more and more of life, observe more and judge less, you become a larger and larger container. You are making room for life and your feelings.

"A Bigger Container" in which to put life means wisdom and compassion naturally grow from seeing life as it is and developing something akin to an unconditional love for life. Acceptance may be the prelude to change. It's easier to take effective action to change something if you're able to accept what's going on. It's paradoxical. Acceptance and becoming "A Bigger Container" give you a firmer foothold in which to deal with slippery slopes.

Take a deep breath. Take a step back. Become awareness. Make room for your feelings. Make room for life.

IT IS WHAT IT IS

If the clouds be full of rain, they empty themselves upon the earth: and if the tree fall toward the South, or toward the North, in the place where the tree falleth, there it shall be.

–Ecclesiastes

Love doesn't conquer all. Good doesn't always prevail over evil. There are unjust wars, and bad things happen to good people. We don't know what's in store for us and it's not easy to sustain peace of mind. Kerry, one of my clients, has reminded me several times that "9/11 started out as a regular day."

Given these less-than-Utopian conditions, how are we supposed to live our lives? Of course, the answer again is as best as we can. That's all you can do. There are Four Noble Truths in Buddhism:

Truth #1: Life is painful because everything changes. All forms, including humans, ruin sooner or later. Painful losses are guaranteed.

Truth #2: The cause of suffering is attachment to how things were. Emotional agony comes from wanting things to be different and not accepting things as they are. It is like wrestling with God.

Truth #3: If you stop craving for life to be other than it is, your suffering, anxiety, and unhappiness will markedly diminish. It's like calling a truce and no longer having an enemy.

Truth #4: If you accept and accommodate change, do no harm by your speech or actions, take responsibility for your behavior and exercise your freedom of choice, do honest work with integrity, and live in the now, giving one-mindedness attention to each moment, your chances of living a meaningful, loving, and happy life greatly increase.

In Buddhism, Truth #4 is called The Eightfold Path and roughly translates to having a roadmap to leading a good life. Almost every religion has its own version of the path. Living the Four Noble Truths is not quite as easy as it may sound. Each day will present you with many opportunities to practice getting better and better. Just because life includes painful experiences, losses, and deaths, and is not particularly fair doesn't mean that we can't help others, enjoy ourselves, matter, love deeply, do good work, and find passion, purpose, meaning, and joy.

After the storm the ocean returned without fanfare to its old offices; the tide climbed onto the snow-covered shore and then receded; so there was the world; sky, water, the pale sand and, where the tide had reached that day's destination, the snow.

And this detail: the body of a duck, a golden-eye; and beside it one black-backed gull. In the body of the duck, among the breast feathers, a hole perhaps an inch across; the color within the hole a shouting red. And bend it as you might, nothing was to blame: storms must toss, and the great black-backed gawker must eat, and so on. It was merely a moment. The sun, angling out from the bunched clouds, cast one could easily imagine tenderly over the landscape its extraordinary light.

–Mary Oliver

Every moment will unfold as it will.
It is what it is.

WHAT IF IT IS?

The great avatar Meher Baba was known for telling his disciples, "Don't worry, be happy." Decades later, Bobby McFerrin penned and performed a song that popularized that expression. Yesterday, I was blessed enough to be able to participate in a spin class with my daughter and my son. During the cooldown at the end of the workout, the instructor played "Don't Worry, Be Happy." She asked the class to sing along. We did. I think everyone felt pretty good.

Don't worry, be happy. An over-simplistic, trite piece of advice or four words of pure cosmic wisdom? You may be surprised that I'm going with the cosmic wisdom choice. We human beings are masters at making things complicated. I am big on parsimony and simplifying, and freedom of choice. You know the old saying to the effect of "you can't walk and chew gum at the same time." Its cousin is "you can't worry and be happy at the same time." They are inversely related.

In *Six Feet Under*, the groundbreaking television series from 2001–2005, an interesting exchange occurs between the dead father and his grown son, David. The father, who died in the first episode, continued to appear in the show for the next five years. He would typically show up to provide some measure of wisdom to his children by helping them see things from a different vantage point. In the final season, Nate (David's brother) dies and David is facing not just the loss of his brother, but also existential despair.

> Father: Don't you get it? You're alive. You can do anything that you want to.
>
> David: It couldn't be that simple.
>
> Father: What if it is?

David would typically worry about many things. His father, who had the luxury of understanding life differently because he was dead, realized how living people make things more complicated than they need be. The father's message was a variant of "Don't worry, be happy." So, which is it? Cosmic wisdom or a trite over-simplification? I'm going to still go with the cosmic wisdom. I know you'll probably say, "It couldn't be that simple." What if it is?

CURIOUS GEORGE

I have a difficult time understanding boredom. It's a big world. There's a lot out there. So much to see. So much to do. So much to learn. So little time. I took an online test having to do with discovering one's strengths. One of my signature strengths is curiosity. The computer printout said that I love learning, find life fascinating, and like exploration and discovery.

> "Two persons met. Over their shoulders hung bags, holding all that they had gathered in the way of their specially fancied treasures on their journeys. No sooner met than they settled themselves there on the ground, spilling out their bags and laying all they'd found out there for the other to see. Excitement was a-growin and their eyes was a-sputterin sparks and there

was laughin and ohin at the other's finds. Soon enough when each had marveled sufficient at the other's gatherins, they put what they'd brought back in their bags and readied to go off on their own ways again. They had a strange way of sayin their farewells. They just took each other's hand and sparked sparks in each other's eyes and laughed mightily like they both knew the same joke and then they walked on off, goin their own ways.

Funny thing happened to em both after that. Wherever each one looked now, they was still a-findin the kind of treasures they had always liked but now they was findin the kind of treasures that other one had liked, too. So the treasures in the world had multiplied for em by two, at least.

And so it went with certain other ones they met, the emptyin of the bag to show the other, eyes a-sparkin into eyes, and the treasures of the world a-doublin and a-triplin and a-buildin up somethin remarkable. Pretty soon there was no way they could look in the world that it wern't brimmin with treasures. You can jest picture what the bags looked like, of all those met in that way. I tell you it was a marvel."

–Kirim

Curiosity and learning are life-enhancing. Being passively entertained can stifle our growth and development. Learning new material as we age seems to produce a better functioning brain. Aside from any physiological benefits that learning may confer, it wakes us up. It's hard to be bored or suffer with ennui when we are actively engaged in learning new material that stimulates our minds and spirits.

> The probability of any of us being here
> is so small that you would think the mere
> fact of existence would keep us all in a
> contented dazzlement of surprise.
> –Lewis Thomas

Einstein had a life long love affair with science and physics. In 1925, he made his last great contribution to quantum mechanics. His biographer, Walter Isaacson, states:

> He would spend the next three decades, ending with some equations scribbled while on his deathbed in 1955, stubbornly criticizing what he regarded as the incompleteness of quantum mechanics while attempting to subsume it into a unified field theory.

By his bedside were 12 pages of equations, including the final line of symbols and numbers he wrote before dying. Einstein did not struggle with boredom.

At a question session with Suzuki Roshi at Sokoji, a young man asked, "What should a Zen practitioner do with his spare time?" Suzuki at first looked perplexed and repeated the phrase, "Spare time?" He repeated it again and then began to laugh uproariously.

–Zen Is Right Here

EXTRAORDINARY WITH OR
WITHOUT THE EXTRA

We're impressed by magic, power, and miracles...and by celebrities...and by the lifestyles of the rich and famous. If you're in a coffee shop having a serious talk with a friend who you're confiding in, the odds are that if Oprah walked in, your friend would immediately shift her focus, attention, and emotion to Oprah and drop your pouring-out heart like a hot potato. Oprah's on TV and you're not.

We're equally unimpressed by the ordinary, the mundane, and the pedestrian. We place little value on the typical day-to-day happenings such as carrying in the groceries, vacuuming, feeding the cat, paying the bills, or weeding the garden. One way I define spirituality is that it's a search for the sacred, for a connection to something extraordinary — something larger than ourselves. Your chances of being happier vastly improve if you have that connection.

Isn't it extraordinary that we're alive? That we exist? That we think and feel and choose? Isn't it extraordinary that there's everything that there is? I'm not only talking about love and chocolate and the Internet. Yes, they're extraordinary. But what about this, that, and the other thing? Have you ever had that aha moment when it becomes clear that all we ever do is go from one extraordinary thing to another? Of course there is illness, loss, heartbreak, and difficulty. Extraordinary is not synonymous with wonderful.

In Zen temples, it is not unusual for the chief monk to do a variety of things. Not only does he impart wisdom via sermons and private meetings, he also sweeps the floors, cleans the toilets, and takes out the garbage. There is no differentiation with regard to how he approaches any or all of the things that he does. Whatever he does, he does whole-heartedly and with his full attention. The sermon is no more holy than sweeping the floor is. It's all grist for the spiritual mill.

> A young student asked the Zen Master, "What did you do before you became Master?"
>
> The Master replied, "I fetched wood and carried water."
>
> The student asked, "What do you do now that you are Master?"
>
> The Master replied, "I fetch wood and carry water."

Is it ordinary or extraordinary that you're alive and hear and see and feel? Is it ordinary or extraordinary that you go where you go and do what you do? That you're free to choose? That you have so many choices? That you …? As far as I'm concerned, ordinary and extraordinary are synonymous.

What is required is surprisingly ordinary:
simply to be who we are where we are,
to subtly shift from *getting somewhere fast*
to *being somewhere completely.*
–Michael Carroll

Zen does not confuse spirituality with
thinking about God while one is peeling potatoes.
Zen spirituality is just to peel the potatoes.
–Alan Watts

How miraculous—
chopping wood,
fetching water.
–Zen haiku

IT'S ALL PART OF THE DANCE

Life is just a bowl of cherries.
–Les Brown

Life is just one damned
thing after another.
–Elbert Hubbard

Life is what you make it.
–Grandma Moses

Birth, beauty, evil, illness, health, elation, sadness, altruism, ego, frustration, death, and serenity—just to name a few. Faith, doubt, the mundane, and the mysterious. It's all part of the dance. Life is a paradox. It can only be exactly as it is at that moment, so the truth of that moment and thus all moments is that life is perfect. And at the same time that the world is perfect, it's also a mess. So what are we to do?

What do we do with war and terrorism, earthquakes that kill 100,000 people, tragedies and catastrophies? How do we deal with loss and pain and our impending deaths? Of course, once again, the answer is as best we can. R.H. Blyth writes that when Thoreau lay dying, he was asked if he had made his peace with God. Thoreau replied, "We have never quarreled."

> Things are as they are and once you
> realize this in its active, not resigned meaning,
> there is nothing really to worry about.
> –R.H. Blyth

It's all part of the dance. We can choose to embrace the dance or sit it out. We can't have our cake and eat it too. We can't have it both ways. If we want the exhilaration, love, beauty, joy, transcendence, and intimacy, we need to accept everything else that comes along with the territory. That's part of the bargain. That's just the way it is. Nothing personal. Remember, Zorba the Greek told us that we have to embrace "the whole catastrophe." The word "amen" translates to "so be it" or "so it is." We need to say amen to life.

Shiva in Judaism refers to a week-long period following a loved one's death in which the close relatives sit together in one place to mourn and receive visitors. Surrounded by family and friends, the mourners sit Shiva to deal with their grief and find the wherewithal to go on with their lives in meaningful ways. It is interesting to me that in Hinduism, Shiva is God represented as a Cosmic Dancer performing a dance called the Tandava. It is a dance in which the universe is created. Hindu art portrays Shiva with one foot atop of a malignant dwarf and the other foot raised in the air as he deals with nature, obstacles, demons, and destructive forces. Throughout it all, Shiva continues to dance. It is a dance of beauty, acceptance, and grace.

We always have the choice of whether to dance or sit it out. Of course, the stumble is part of the dance. So is the fall. So is the getting up again — as many times as you have to.

> Over the years, I have seen the power of taking an unconditional relationship to life. I am surprised to have found a sort of willingness to show up for whatever life may offer and meet with it rather than wishing to edit and change the inevitable.
> –Rachel Naomi Remen

Enjoy as much as you can for as long as you can by switching to a very wide-angle lens and seeing clearly — maybe for the first time — that it's all part of the dance.

Kick off your shoes and dance.

APPENDIX A:
POSITIVE PSYCH 101

Seligman has outlined six ubiquitous virtues that are found in virtually every culture in the world. They are the backbone of religious, ethical, and philosophical traditions. The virtues are:

–Wisdom and Knowledge
–Courage
–Love and Humanity
–Justice
–Temperance
–Spirituality and Transcendence

The 6 virtues noted above are comprised of 24 measurable character strengths. As you proceed to read descriptions of all 24 signature strengths below, rate/circle yourself on a scale of 1 to 10, with 1 being the least representative of you and 10 being the most:

Wisdom and Knowledge

Curiosity, Interest in the world
You're open to new experiences and like to take a flexible approach to most things. You don't just tolerate ambiguity; you're intrigued by it. Your curiosity involves a wide-eyed approach to the world and a desire to actively engage in novelty.

That's not me!   Definitely me!
| 1 | 2 | 3 | 4 | 5 | 6 | 7 | 8 | 9 | 10 |

Love of Learning
You love learning new things. You love being an expert and/or being in a position where your knowledge is valued by others.

That's not me!   Definitely me!
| 1 | 2 | 3 | 4 | 5 | 6 | 7 | 8 | 9 | 10 |

Judgment, Critical Thinking, Open Mindedness
It's important to you to think things through and to examine issues from all angles. You don't quickly jump to conclusions but instead, carefully weigh evidence to make decisions. If the facts suggest you've been wrong in the past, you'll easily change your mind.

That's not me!   Definitely me!
| 1 | 2 | 3 | 4 | 5 | 6 | 7 | 8 | 9 | 10 |

Ingenuity, Originality, Practical Intelligence
You excel in finding new and different ways to approach problems and/or to achieve your goals. You rarely settle for simply doing things the conventional way, more often looking to find better and more effective approaches.

That's not me!   Definitely me!

<u>1   2   3   4   5   6   7   8   9   10</u>

Social and Emotional Intelligence
You have a good understanding of yourself and of others. You are aware of your own moods and how to manage them. You're also very good at judging the moods of others and responding appropriately to their needs.

That's not me!   Definitely me!

<u>1   2   3   4   5   6   7   8   9   10</u>

Perspective
This strength is a form of wisdom. Others seek you out to draw on your ability to effectively solve problems and gain perspective. You have a way of looking at the world that makes sense and is helpful to yourself and to others.

That's not me!   Definitely me!

<u>1   2   3   4   5   6   7   8   9   10</u>

Courage

Valour, Bravery
You're prepared to take on challenges, and deal with difficult situations even if unpopular or dangerous. You have the courage to overcome fear as well as ability to take a moral stance under stressful circumstances.

That's not me!   Definitely me!
1   2   3   4   5   6   7   8   9   10

Perseverance, Diligence, Industry
You finish what you start. You're industrious and prepared to take on difficult projects (and you finish them). You do what you say and sometimes you even do more.

That's not me!   Definitely me!
1   2   3   4   5   6   7   8   9   10

Integrity, Honesty
You're honest, speaking the truth as well as living your life in a genuine and authentic way. You're down to earth and without pretense.

That's not me!   Definitely me!
1   2   3   4   5   6   7   8   9   10

Humanity and Love

Kindness, Generosity
You're kind and generous to others, and never too busy

to do a favor. You gain pleasure and joy from doing good deeds for others. In fact, your actions are often guided by other people's best interests. At the core of this particular strength is an acknowledgement of the worth of others.

That's not me!   Definitely me!

| 1 | 2 | 3 | 4 | 5 | 6 | 7 | 8 | 9 | 10 |

Loving, Being Loved

You place a high value on close and intimate relationships with others. More than just loving and caring for others, they feel the same way about you and you allow yourself to be loved.

That's not me!   Definitely me!

| 1 | 2 | 3 | 4 | 5 | 6 | 7 | 8 | 9 | 10 |

Justice

Citizenship, Loyalty, Teamwork

You're a great team player, excelling as a member of a group. You are loyal and dedicated to your colleagues, always contributing your share and working hard for the good and success of the group.

That's not me!   Definitely me!

| 1 | 2 | 3 | 4 | 5 | 6 | 7 | 8 | 9 | 10 |

Fairness, Equity

You do not allow your own personal feelings to bias your

decisions about other people. Instead, you give everyone a fair go and are guided by your larger principles of morality.

That's not me!   Definitely me!

| 1 | 2 | 3 | 4 | 5 | 6 | 7 | 8 | 9 | 10 |

Leadership
You're a good organizer and you're good at making sure things happen. You ensure work is completed by you and also maintain good relationships among group members.

That's not me!   Definitely me!

| 1 | 2 | 3 | 4 | 5 | 6 | 7 | 8 | 9 | 10 |

Temperance

Self-Control
You can easily keep your desires, needs and impulses in check when necessary or appropriate. As well as knowing what's correct, you're able to put this knowledge into action.

That's not me!   Definitely me!

| 1 | 2 | 3 | 4 | 5 | 6 | 7 | 8 | 9 | 10 |

Discretion, Caution, Prudence
You're a careful person. You look before you leap. You rarely, if ever, say or do things you later regret. You typically wait until all options have been fully considered before embarking on any course of action. You look ahead

and deliberate carefully, making sure long-term success takes precedence over shorter-term goals.

That's not me!   Definitely me!

1	2	3	4	5	6	7	8	9	10

Modesty, Humility

You don't seek or want the spotlight. You're happy for your accomplishments to speak for themselves but you don't ever seek to be the center of attention. You don't necessarily see yourself as being special and others often comment on, and respect your modesty.

That's not me!   Definitely me!

1	2	3	4	5	6	7	8	9	10

Transcendence

Appreciation of beauty and excellence

You're one of those people who stops to smell the roses. You appreciate beauty, excellence and skill.

That's not me!   Definitely me!

1	2	3	4	5	6	7	8	9	10

Gratitude

You are highly aware of all the good things that happen to you and you never take them for granted. Further, you take time to express your thanks and you appreciate the goodness in others.

That's not me!   Definitely me!

| 1 | 2 | 3 | 4 | 5 | 6 | 7 | 8 | 9 | 10 |

Hope, Optimism

You expect the best for the future and you plan and work to achieve it. Your focus is on the future and on a positive future at that. You know that if you set goals and work hard, good things will happen.

That's not me!   Definitely me!

| 1 | 2 | 3 | 4 | 5 | 6 | 7 | 8 | 9 | 10 |

Spirituality, Faith, Sense of Purpose

You have strong and coherent beliefs about the higher purpose and meaning of the world. You're also aware of your position in this world and in the larger scheme of things. This awareness shapes your beliefs, which shape your daily actions; this is a strong source of comfort to you.

That's not me!   Definitely me!

| 1 | 2 | 3 | 4 | 5 | 6 | 7 | 8 | 9 | 10 |

Forgiveness, Mercy

If you're wronged, you can forgive. You allow people a second chance. You're guided more by mercy than revenge.

That's not me!   Definitely me!

| 1 | 2 | 3 | 4 | 5 | 6 | 7 | 8 | 9 | 10 |

Playfulness, Humor

You like to laugh and to make others laugh and smile. You enjoy and are good at play. You easily see the light side of life.

That's not me!   Definitely me!

| 1 | 2 | 3 | 4 | 5 | 6 | 7 | 8 | 9 | 10 |

Passion, Enthusiasm

You're energetic, spirited and passionate. You wake up and look forward to most days. You throw yourself, body and soul, into all activities you undertake.

That's not me!   Definitely me!

| 1 | 2 | 3 | 4 | 5 | 6 | 7 | 8 | 9 | 10 |

Adapted from the work of Professor Martin Seligman

Take your five highest ratings. These are your unique signature strengths. The idea is for you to take them and run with them, so to speak, utilizing these strengths every day in your work, your family, your relationships, and your pursuits. Being aware of and consciously using your signature strengths should increase your confidence and well-being, and help you to feel happier and live the good and meaningful life.

My top five signature strengths are gratitude, self-control, hope and optimism, curiosity and interest in the world, and perseverance and diligence. In fact, I almost always feel grateful, choose carefully what feelings I want to act on, am your card-carrying eternal optimist, am fascinated by the world, and regularly take on and complete difficult projects and challenges. My signature strengths provide an accurate picture and guideline for me with regard to approaching my life. I utilize those strengths at home, at work, at play, and in life in general.

Take your signature strengths and run with them.

PERMISSIONS

Thank you to Short Books for permission to use material from *Going Buddhist* by Peter J. Conradi.

Thank you to Power Press for permission to use the story of Max's Sandwich Shop from *Zen and the Art of Happiness* by Chris Prentiss.

Thank you to Beacon Press for permission to use poetry from Mary Oliver that was in *New and Selected Poems, Volume II*.

Thank you to The McGraw-Hill Companies for permission to use material from *Happier* by Tal Ben-Shahar, Ph.D.

Thank you to Shambhala for permission to use material from *Zen Is Right Here* by David Chadwick.

Thank you to The Overlook Press for permission to use the poem "Coffee With Milk" from *Top of My Lungs* by Natalie Goldberg.

Thank you to Simon & Schuster, Inc., for permission to use the time management matrix graph from Stephen R. Covey's *The 7 Habits of Highly Effective People*.

Thank you to Harper Collins Publishers for permission to use the poem "The Invitation" from the book of the same name by Oriah Mountain Dreamer.

Thank you to Harper Collins Publishers for permission to use material from *It's Easier Than You Think: The Buddhist Way to Happiness* by Sylvia Boorstein.

Thank you to World Wisdom, Inc., for permission to use a passage by Sushila Blackman, which originally appeared in John C.H. Wu's *The Golden Age of Zen*.

Thank you to thehappinessinstitute.com for permission to use information printed in this book.

NOTES

Wikipedia.com was utilized in obtaining certain information related to:

> The End of the World
> Occam's Razor
> Eos
> Six Degrees of Separation
> Pyrrhic Victory
> Reframing

If you would like to send a donation to the Darryl Anne Burnham Memorial Fund, please send a check payable to Elisabeth Morrow School and write Darryl Anne Burnham Memorial Fund on the check. Checks may be mailed to:

Alan Gettis, Ph.D.

Elisabeth Morrow School
435 Lydecker Street
Englewood, NJ 07631

Donations can also be made online at:
elisabethmorrow.org/supporting_ems/endowment_funds/index.aspx

REFERENCES

Adams, Douglas. <u>The Hitchhiker's Guide to the Galaxy</u>. New York: Ballantine Books, 1995.

Bayda, Ezra and Josh Bartok. <u>Saying Yes to Life (Even the Hard Parts)</u>. Somerville: Wisdom Publications, 2005.

Beck, Charlotte Joko. <u>Everyday Zen: Love and Work</u>. San Francisco: Harper and Row, 1989.

Ben-Shahar, Tal. <u>Happier</u>. New York: McGraw Hill, 2007.

Blackman, Sushila. <u>Graceful Exits: How Great Beings Die – Death Stories of Hindu, Tibetan, Buddhist, and Zen Masters</u>. Boston: Shambhala, 1997.

Blyth, R.H. <u>Zen and Zen Classics, Volume Two</u>. Tokyo: The Hokuseido Press, 1976.

Blyth, R.H. <u>Zen and Zen Classics, Volume Four</u>. Tokyo: The Hokuseido Press, 1978.

Blyth, R.H. <u>Zen and Zen Classics, Volume Five</u>. Tokyo: The Hokuseido Press, 1966.

Boorstein, Sylvia. <u>It's Easier Than You Think: The Buddhist Way to Happiness</u>. San Francisco: Harper Collins, 1997.

Buell, Hal. <u>Moments: The Pulitzer Prize-Winning Photographs</u>. New York: Tess Press, 2007.

Campbell, Joseph. <u>The Masks of God: Primitive Mythology</u>. New York: Penguin Books, 1984.

Castaneda, Carlos. <u>Journey to Ixtlan</u>. New York: Washington Square Press, 1992.

Chadwick, David. <u>Zen Is Right Here</u>. Boston: Shambhala, 2007.

Conradi, Peter J. "The Mystic and the Cynic." In M. McLeod's (ed.) <u>The Best Buddhist Writing 2006</u>. Shambhala, 2006.

<u>Contact</u>. DVD. Warner Home Video, 1997.

Covey, Stephen R. <u>The 7 Habits of Highly Effective People</u>. New York: Fireside, 1990.

Dass, Ram. <u>Grist For the Mill</u>. Santa Cruz: Unity Press, 1977.

Emmons, Robert A. and Michael E. McCullough. <u>The Psychology of Gratitude</u>. New York: Oxford University Press, 2004.

Emoto, Masaru. <u>The Hidden Messages in Water</u>. New York: Atria Books, 2004.

Erdoes, Richard and Alfonso Ortiz. <u>American Indian Myths and Legends</u>. New York: Pantheon, 1984.

Gettis, Alan. <u>Seven Times Down, Eight Times Up: Landing On Your Feet in an Upside Down World - Second Edition, Updated and Expanded</u>. Norwood: Goodman Beck Publishing, 2009.

Gettis, Alan. <u>Sun Faced Haiku, Moon Faced Haiku</u>. Battle Ground: High/Coo Press, 1982.

Gettis, Alan. <u>The Happiness Solution: Finding Joy and Meaning in an Upside Down World</u>. Norwood: Goodman Beck Publishing, 2008.

Gettis, Alan. "The Jesus Delusion: A Theoretical and Phenomenological Look." <u>Journal of Religion and Health</u>. 26.2 (1987): 131-136.

Gettis, Alan. "Psychotherapy as Exorcism." <u>Journal of Religion and Health</u> 15.3 (1976): 188-190.

Goldberg, Natalie. <u>Top of My Lungs</u>. Woodstock: The Overlook Press, 2002.

Goleman, Daniel. "Hardwired For Altruism." In M. McLeod's (ed.) <u>The Best Buddhist Writing 2007</u>. Shambhala, 2007.

Gordon, Jon. <u>The Energy Bus: 10 Rules to Fuel Your Life, Work, and Team With Positive Energy</u>. Hoboken: Wiley, 2007.

Harris, Russ. <u>The Happiness Trap</u>. Boston: Shambhala, 2008.

Henig, Robin Marantz. "Darwin's God." <u>The New York Times</u>. 4 March 2007.

Hyde, Catherine Ryan. <u>Pay It Forward</u>. New York: Simon & Schuster, 2000.

Isaacson, Walter. <u>Einstein: His Life and Universe</u>. New York: Simon & Schuster, 2007.

Jordan, Meredith. <u>Embracing the Mystery: The Sacred Unfolding in Ordinary People and Everyday Lives</u>. Biddeford: Rogers McKay, 2004.

Kushner, Harold S. <u>When Bad Things Happen to Good People</u>. New York: Avon, 1983.

Livingston, Gordon. <u>And Never Stop Dancing</u>. New York: Marlowe & Co., 2006.

Maddi, Salvatore R. "The Courage and Strategies of Hardiness as Helpful in Growing Despite Major, Disruptive Stresses." <u>American Psychologist</u> 63.6 (2008): 563-564.

MacPhillamy, Daizui. "A Path of Radical Sobriety." In M. McLeod's (ed.) <u>The Best Buddhist Writing 2004</u>. Shambhala, 2004.

Matthews, Andrew. <u>Being Happy: A Handbook to Greater Confidence and Security</u>. Los Angeles: Price Stern Sloan, 1990.

May, Rollo. <u>Freedom and Destiny</u>. New York: Norton, 1981.

Miller, Michael Vincent. "After the Beginning." <u>O, The Oprah Magazine</u>. Feb. 2006. <http://www.oprah.com/article/omagazine/omag_200602_beginning>.

McLeod, Melvin. <u>The Best Buddhist Writing 2007</u>. Boston: Shambhala, 2007.

McLeod, Melvin. <u>The Best Buddhist Writing 2006</u>. Boston: Shambhala, 2006.

McLeod, Melvin. <u>The Best Buddhist Writing 2005</u>. Boston: Shambhala, 2005.

McLeod, Melvin. <u>The Best Buddhist Writing 2004</u>. Boston: Shambhala, 2004.

Oliver, Mary. <u>New and Selected Poems: Volume Two</u>. Boston: Beacon Press, 2005.

Oliver, Mary: <u>Thirst</u>. Boston: Beacon Press, 2006.

Osbon, Diane K. <u>A Joseph Campbell Companion</u>. New York: Harper Collins, 1991.

Pollan, Stephen M. and Mark Levine. <u>It's All in Your Head: Thinking Your Way to Happiness</u>. New York: Collins, 2005.

Prentiss, Chris. <u>Zen and the Art of Happiness</u>. Malibu: Power Press, 2006.

Reed, Lou. "Dime Store Mystery." <u>New York</u>. Rhino, 1990.

Remen, Rachel Naomi. <u>Kitchen Table Wisdom</u>. New York: Penguin, 2006.

Remen, Rachel Naomi. <u>My Grandfather's Blessings</u>. New York: Riverhead Books, 2000.

Safford, Victoria. "Opening Words." <u>UU World</u>. Fall 2008: 1.

Sagan, Carl. <u>Contact</u>. New York: Pocket, 1997.

Sartre, Jean-Paul. <u>Nausea</u>. New York: New Directions, 1964.

Steinbeck, John. <u>Travels with Charley in Search of America</u>. New York: Penguin, 1997.

Suzuki, Shunryu. <u>Zen Is Right Here</u>. Boston: Shambhala, 2007.

Tennyson, Alfred Lord. <u>Everyman's Poetry</u>. London: Orion, 2004.

Wade, Nicholas. "Scientist Finds the Beginnings of Morality in Primate Behavior." <u>The New York Times</u>. 20 March 2007.

Warner, Brad. "Everything Confirmed in an Instant." In M. McLeod's (ed.) <u>The Best Buddhist Writing 2004</u>. Shambhala, 2004.

Weil, Andrew. <u>Healthy Aging: A Lifelong Guide to Your Physical and Spiritual Well-Being</u>. New York: Alfred A. Knopf, 2005.

Williamson, Marianne. <u>Return to Love: Reflections On the Principles of a Course in Miracles</u>. New York: Harper Collins, 1996.

ABOUT THE AUTHOR

Dr. Alan Gettis is a clinical psychologist steeped in cognitive behavioral psychotherapy, positive psychology, and Zen. He continues his psychotherapy private practice that he began 35 years ago. He uses storytelling as a vehicle to help people remove obstacles to their happiness. This is his fifth book. His previous book, *The Happiness Solution: Finding Joy and Meaning in an Upside Down World*, was selected as the best psychology/mental health book of the year by USA Book News. It was also chosen as one of the "Top Ten Books of the Year" by The Best You Can Be Foundation, which honors books that make a significant difference in people's lives. For more information about Dr. Gettis, please visit drgettis.com.